S

TOOLS

for

SPEAKING AND SINGING

by

GERTRUDE WHEELER BECKMAN, *1879–*

G. SCHIRMER, Inc.

New York

Plates

Drawn by Carl Hague

If music means much to you and if you have an urge to sing — you can! No one else can touch the instrument within you. You and you only are the *real teacher,* and there must be no doubt whatever about your way of procedure.

Singing is each individual's personal discovery, and this book impels you on to that fascinating task by presenting you with the necessary tools.

Devotedly inscribed,

GERTRUDE WHEELER BECKMAN

iii

CONTENTS

PART I

v

PART II

How to Use the Tools for Speaking and Singing

TOOLS FOR SPEAKING AND SINGING

CHAPTER ONE

THE WAY OF A DISCOVERER

Great people of all times have possessed an instinctive physical resiliency and, as a natural corollary, mental elasticity. These are the people who have obeyed Nature's laws throughout their lives. Actually their very destiny is so interwoven with primal Principle that they could not create without it.

Singers who consciously or unconsciously set up these same physical conditions from which resiliency emanates are the people who "let the singing get done *through* them" instead of *by* them. They breathe naturally instead of painstakingly trying to "manage" a portion of their inside anatomy known as the "diaphragm." They are even unconscious of a throat. Instead of trying to master larynx, pharynx, soft palate and tongue, they are unaware of this complicated mechanism. To them the back of the throat is a sleeping thing, never changing its shape throughout the entire singing range. Only when such conditions are set up and continuously maintained can the

1

creative impulse of the true artist become one with that of the composer and poet. To quote from a letter written by Ida Auer-Herbeck in 1906: "In this way the body pulls itself together for the expression of the soul, thereby revealing the singing instrument and the management thereof that leads to great natural voice expression."

Many years ago my own great teacher, Ida Auer-Herbeck (whom I have to thank for my initiation into vocal research), told me the story of her unique and very' personal vocal experience. Since then I have often passed it on to my own pupils in the course of my teaching. Its never-failing helpfulness has convinced me that it is worthy of being put into a more lasting form. It is actually the story of one person's discovery of the needed "tools for singing," but that story must be more or less re-experienced by each seeker after the truth about voice education.

In the autumn of 1904, when I first went to Ida Auer-Herbeck, she was close to sixty. She was born, then, sometime during the middle 1840's in Lyons, France. Her family returned to their native south Germany when she was sixteen, and her musical education, begun in early childhood, continued at the conservatory in Munich. Peter Cornelius taught her harmony and theory, and Julius Hey trained her voice. Hey had written many books on singing and speaking and was considered the greatest authority in Germany on these subjects.

Ida must have had a lovely lyric soprano from the beginning, but her voice had one inherent fault which Hey, though recognizing it only too well, seemed totally unable to eradicate. The voice was smooth and even from its lowest tone up to B, third line. Then, after C, it was equally beautiful and unbroken up to almost indefinite heights. But the two tones in the middle, B and C, were dull, breathy, lacking in ring and resonance. "Diese zwei Töne, die *müssen* herauskommen! Die *müssen* herauskommen!"[1] Hey would shriek, pounding the piano as he did so. The little girl (she was very small) would

---

[1] "These two tones, they *must* come out! They *must* come out!"

take a big breath and push with all her might. But try as she would, those two stubborn tones, B and C, refused to leave their hiding place.

Ida's problem was by no means uncommon, and like many a singer with a similar defect she camouflaged it for a few precarious years. Beginning her operatic career[2] at the age of eighteen, Ida skilfully concealed her vocal imperfection by rephrasing or sudden pianissimo. But the break in her voice failed to improve. It was like a spot of decay in an otherwise perfect piece of fruit. A miserable home life only aggravated the situation. Then the inevitable happened. Her voice went to pieces and she was forced to leave the stage after a career of eight years.

What could she do? Where could she go for help? She had been trained by a teacher of the highest calibre. Evidently he had failed.

The future seemed dark indeed, but there was one ray of hope in the shape of a colossal, jolly soul named Karl Planck. Planck's story was well known to Ida. He was one of her colleagues at the opera, and I have heard her say that he was the greatest Wotan she had ever heard or could expect to hear. That he cut a ridiculous figure was quite evident from the photograph of him that stood upon her piano many years after. His face couldn't help being merry. He had thick, straight, black hair, snapping black eyes, a mouth curved up at the corners in the pleasantest of Cupid's bows, and I don't remember how many chins hanging comfortably beneath. Auer-

---

[2] Though short, she was perfectly proportioned, and she possessed the majesty of bearing that caused her always to dominate the stage no matter how many people shared it with her. This was told me by an old lady who had heard "die Herbeck" many times at the Karlsruh Theater and the Prinz Regenten Theater in Munich. Auer-Herbeck's full title was "Grossherzogliche Badische Hofopernsängerin." In her studio in Dresden, where she later taught, there hung charming old pictures of herself in various roles. Several, I especially recall, showed her as Cherubino in *The Marriage of Figaro,* her perfect little limbs encased in doublet and hose. Her round face, too, was pretty and entirely Germanic — large, very blue eyes and a small, sensitive mouth. She married in her early twenties, and it was a most unhappy affair. The one son who resulted from this union later became a well known Berlin editor.

Herbeck insisted that his weight was somewhere between three and four hundred pounds. He looked like a circus character or "Peck's Bad Boy."

His vocal history had been strange indeed. He had a natural voice of tremendous range. Auer-Herbeck used to say that when she knew him in the theater, his voice extended over four octaves. It was decided by his teachers that he was destined to be that *rara avis,* a genuine heroic tenor, and as such he made his début.

After a few years as a tenor, however, Planck's voice began to deteriorate. He left the stage to work alone on his problem. When ready, he returned to the opera — as a baritone — and remained the greatest in Germany until he died.[3]

Auer-Herbeck was perhaps correct in her estimate that but for his absurd proportions, he would have been known the world over as the greatest baritone of his day. His must have been a voice like that of Battistini, who lived a generation later.

It seems singular that having gone through the deep human experience of first losing then finding his voice, he was wholly unable to describe this metamorphosis! He used to say: "I cannot tell you how I do it. I only know it is right."

He had a large group of pupils, but could teach them nothing, according to Auer-Herbeck. He was a kind and friendly person, however, and told "the little Herbeck" she could come to his studio and watch him whenever she liked. She went faithfully, and it proved to be the turning point in her life as an artist and a teacher.

She has told me that Planck was unbelievably light on his feet. (Having seen Paul Whiteman, I can well understand it.) He would come dancing into the room in the gayest of moods, announcing:

---

[3] Planck finally met an untimely end by falling from an improperly secured scaffolding in the theater, while singing the title role in *The Flying Dutchman.* An autopsy was duly performed at the instigation of the insurance company. Auer-Herbeck considered the results amazing. Not an ounce of excess fat was found within his body. His singing and consequent deep breathing had thrown it entirely to the *outside* body!

"Listen to this! I have just now invented the loveliest exercise for the vocal cords!" Then he would burst into an elaborate roulade, running the gamut of his phenomenal range. He spoke of singing only in terms of vocal cords, because the rest of his great body (head included) functioned exactly as it should and hence failed to make itself evident to him.

But Ida Auer-Herbeck knew very well that thinking and talking about *vocal cords* would never help her case. There must be a *cause* somehow, somewhere, that was responsible for the behavior of Planck's vocal cords in the exercises through which he so joyously put them. This cause she now set out to find.

I don't know how long it was after she had begun to study and observe Planck as a vocal machine, but one day the thought suddenly struck her that the small part of our anatomy called the throat, containing the still smaller larynx, was not segregated, accountable only to itself for its behavior. Instead, throat and larynx depended directly upon the behavior of the chest below them. Nor, in turn, was the chest independent. It depended upon the action of the shoulder blades. If the shoulder blades parted company, they became a burden upon the falling chest, and direct support for throat and head promptly ceased. Yes, Planck's shoulder blades remained supple, flat, actively seeking each other, whether he inhaled or exhaled, and *for that reason* his great chest was always high!

But the entire thorax section of his body — upon what did *that* depend? It certainly wasn't hanging in mid-air! Structurally it was connected to that other big "cross-beam" section, the pelvis (or "basin" as the Germans descriptively term it), by the spinal column. A sinking-in at this point, a "sway-back," gave people clumsy figures and protruding stomachs. Not so Planck, for all his surplus weight. The inward curves of his spine at the neck and in the lumbar region, so exaggerated in most people, were almost straight. His enormous back seemed to be a unit, generating endless power.

Yet even that back depended upon something else, something

below, Ida reasoned. Those dancing legs and feet! Whenever he sang, even though he stood in one spot, there seemed to be a stream of pulsing activity starting at the very floor and coursing through his entire body. The heel of one foot and the toe of the other dug into the floor as though he were about to walk, getting a rebound above in exact proportion to that dig.

So the subject of singing was not something related to one or two or even three sections of the body. It was a matter of *interdependence and balance*—one part relying upon another directly below it, beginning with the head and going down to the very feet. The *entire body* worked together in a state of harmonious activity. In this manner the part above the collar bones remained supported, the throat continued open and changeless, while breathing—inhaling and exhaling—went on automatically.

She realized for the first time that singing was a question of unity, of sensing a vital *pull*—a plumb line stretching through the human instrument from feet to head. If bouncing Karl Planck should cease for one moment to maintain that *pull,* then the front portion of his body (the soft part) would collapse, his breathing would cease to function properly, and the throat would close.

All this Ida Auer-Herbeck saw in one consistent and tremendous vision, and from that moment she was convinced of its soundness. She went home on that memorable day determined to put it into practice. Then followed a strange, absorbing fortnight.

The great thing to bear in mind, she felt, was that a fundamental approach underlies every desirable result in beautiful singing. She would concern herself solely with fundamentals, no matter what the immediate results might be.

The immediate results were comical and baffling. She tried to sing a simple scale. No voice came—just a breathy whisper! Even the little that remained after so many years of vocal wrongdoing had vanished, leaving nothing but chaos. Then it was that Ida Auer-Herbeck made a declaration to herself which has always represented for me the height of courage: "Es macht mir garnichts aus ob ich eine Stimme bekomme oder nicht—auf diesem *Wege,* aber, muss ich gehen bis zum Ende!"[4]

But the coordination of her body from head to toe—how could she achieve that harmonious activity, that happy, easy working-together of the *whole* body, the complete singing instrument with nothing omitted? Planck's perfect abandon and at the same time perfect control puzzled her.

Ida now considered the action of animals and birds. Her canary stretched from beak to tail *before* beginning its song and maintained that stretch until *after* the last note. His likeness to Planck was striking. She remembered a farmer's pertinent remark: a certain rooster that persisted in crowing regularly at two o'clock must be stopped at once by raising the henhouse perch so high that he couldn't stretch and crane his neck!

Of course, she thought, nature demanded of every creature a special coordination that it might become articulate in its own way. Animals were relaxed whether asleep or awake, and when they became vocal, a vital power seemed to activate them by stretching *through* their relaxation. They needed no knowledge of diaphragms and open throats and raised palates, yet these organs apparently functioned flawlessly.

Next Ida considered human perfection in a healthy infant. Many a time had she heard Julius Hey and other voice authorities agree that babies had the secret of correct breathing; yet, she reasoned, babies *knew* nothing whatever about the subject! *They* didn't "do" the breathing. Maybe that was the secret. Maybe the singer's attitude should be that of the baby—not to "manage" the diaphragm or to "open" the throat or "raise" the soft palate—indeed, not to *do* the breathing or even the singing, but to *let all these things get done through him.*

---

[4] "It makes no difference to me whether I ever get a voice or not — but this *path* I must follow to the end."

When Nature has done her work so perfectly, how dare we adults think that we can improve matters by *bossing the job* of breathing and speaking and singing? No, we are only throwing sand into the machinery, committing vocal sabotage. The one thing we *can* do to help is to get in line with Nature and cooperate with her by becoming children again. Becoming, as a little child means having the same set-up and *feeling* that a child has. There is nothing more relaxed than a sleeping infant. If it could tell us *how* it feels, I venture to say the word "heavy" would be a perfect description. A dog or cat at rest would agree with the baby. But when the baby is awake, he is immediately charged with abounding vitality. We call him a "bouncing baby." He is still completely relaxed. In fact, it is *because* he is relaxed that he *can* be so full of the living thing. He crows or cries, and his chest never falls. His diaphragm functions perfectly, yet he doesn't know he possesses one! Heaviness, relaxation, is being continually lifted and tossed about by the power of·life itself.

That way of looking at it might explain Karl Planck's failure to mention diaphragm, open throat, etc. It even suggested a reason for his inarticulateness: "I cannot tell you *how* I do it. I only know it is the right way to sing."

In the peculiar metamorphosis which Ida now found herself entering, she decided that to begin at the very beginning she must start with the relaxation of babies and animals. To her amazement she found she knew very little about the subject. She had heard wise ones say: "Of course it is right to relax *up to a certain point*. If you go beyond that you will fall to the floor!" She came to the conclusion that this reasoning was false, that she was either relaxed or stiff, and that there was no compromise between the two "at a certain point."

To prove her case she set herself tasks quite divorced from singing as such. For instance, she "slumped" in a straight-backed chair, feeling supremely heavy. Then she decided to lift this heavy "lump" up out of the chair. Simultaneously she sensed the pulling and stretching of a line throughout the lump, from the suddenly vital, pushing feet to the top of the head. When she let go this imaginary cord, the lump would again slump together on the chair. She repeated this perform-ance many times—stretching, slumping, pulling, and letting go the string. She felt rather like a jumping jack in the hands of a child.

Rising to her feet was a real struggle. She fought an almost irresistible desire to "help" by throwing her weight forward—what everyone does a hundred times a day in the ordinary process of standing up. If she did this, she at once lost the sensation of an unbroken pull, the feeling of great weight and at the same time equally great power. She forced herself to keep her weight back, and presently discovered that the same pull from the firmly planted feet would carry her on up until she was standing. But what a strange new sensation! Never had she felt so light on her feet, and she felt very tall indeed. It was as though she were ready to accomplish anything she might elect to do.

Why not try to sing while this wonderful feeling of freedom lasted? She experimented with her voice through a limited range. She tried very hard *not to try,* but to let the singing get done through her undirected body. The only demand she allowed her ear to make was that every vowel sound should be clear and crude and bright, like a baby beginning to talk—not "prettified"—and that the pitch should be what she ordered. Some sounds actually came through—strange animal sounds that she had never before heard herself make. But though she rocked with laughter at these first crude results, she refused to alter them. She had started upon a way from which there was no turning. "And anyhow," she reasoned, "*I* am not making these weird noises, so I am not responsible for their lack of beauty! I am merely ordering certain vowels and certain pitches, and I insist upon main-taining this new feeling that started with my getting up from the chair! That is all I can concentrate on at the present moment. So I will *not* concern myself with beauty or lack of beauty. At least I *feel* as though I have no throat at all when sounds 'come through' in this strange fashion. I like this feeling of not feeling, and I intend to maintain it and see where it leads, for I sense a whole new world ahead waiting to be discovered, and this is only the very beginning. All good beginnings are crude, and I won't demand a finished article from this new, struggling machine!"

So obsessed was Ida by her clear-sighted vision that she worked every day and all day. There was no standing still. Each day brought its treasure of experience to be stored up and later given to the world.

Out of the chaos that had once been a lovely soprano, a "born voice," there evolved gradually, unhurriedly and spottily, a few tones here, one or two there, a singing instrument which, when it had pieced itself together by the end of that eventful fortnight, was as beautiful and as perfect as one could wish to hear.

I heard her only in her old age, in her studio, and I rejoice in bearing witness to the fact that in 1904-6 her voice was as fresh as though she were eighteen. Her trill was perfect—both tones in flawless tune, a phenomenon generally confined to orchestral instruments.

Ida Auer-Herbeck's true mission in life was now very clear. It was to pass on to a waiting world this revolutionary idea concerning voice production. Now she could understand why Planck could not describe his own experience. Her own life during that thrilling fortnight seemed like a consuming conflagration. How could she ever describe its details to young students who might come her way? Ida struggled with that problem the rest of her life.

She was now absolutely certain of herself and of her voice— "secure in my insecurity," as she paradoxically called it. She could hardly wait to show Planck the result of her two weeks of research. He was utterly delighted, declaring, "Now, my child, at last you're beginning to sing!" He lost no time in opening his copy of *Don Juan* to the duet "Reich mir die Hand," which they had performed numberless times in past years at the Opera. Together they sang Mozart as never before.

Ida Auer-Herbeck never considered returning to opera. She heard a far more insistent call to a wider, deeper field—one that had been waiting ever since the Golden Age of Italian song—the field of teaching. Here she was destined for disappointment, which only increased as the years went on. She had brought a new truth to the world, and the world had no wish to receive it! Instead, it continued complacently unaware of its need, and young singers still asked for bread, only to be given stones. Many voices were ruined, and it was her lot to build her class from these.

"If only I had some of the wonderful unspoiled talent — the American talent—that streams to the studios of S— and O— and I—!" she would complain, referring to three popular teachers. "They only come to me as a last resort, after their voices and hearts are broken, and alas, their pocketbooks as well!"

Towards the close of the century she was called to teach at the Royal Conservatory in Dresden. She gave an amusing account of her conversation with the principal:

He: Mme. Auer, what method do you teach?

She: I teach the right way to sing.

He: But what is your method? People want a name! Is it then the German method? Or the Italian method? Or the French method?

She: The right way to sing is the only method to teach, whether you find it in France or in Germany or in Italy or in the heart of Africa. The right way to sing cannot be localized. It belongs to all people who want it and find it, no matter where they may be.

He: I think I see your point, Madame. But still the people will demand a name. What do you wish us to say to them?

She: If the people *must* have a name for the way I teach, then call it the old, old, *old* Italian method—not the modern Italian method! From what I have been able to gather through research and from reading the scant literature left to the world by the great Italian masters of the 17th and 18th centuries, my ideas and my ways are closest to theirs.

This shows how Auer-Herbeck disliked the use of the word "method" in voice education. I can remember her using it only once, in speaking of her work: "Meine Methode ist selbstgefunden." ("My method is original—self-found."[5])

---

[5] In Sweden in the summer of 1913 we sat together in a fairylike garden. Her health was frail, and she, who so many years before had set forth upon her destined road with zeal and high courage, was now a sad little old woman, bitter with disappointment. She laid a hand on my knee and I looked into her upturned face; tears streamed from her eyes as she said, "Gertrude, now I know that I must die without having established my ideas in this world, where the need is so desperate!"

I begged her to take some comfort in the thought that I would carry on to the best of my ability — that I would never let the torch fall. I think she scarcely heard me, she was so completely preoccupied with her own gloomy outlook. And I must have seemed anything but a promising Guardian and Promulgator of the Truth about Singing! A growing young family seemed almost a guarantee that serious teaching and deep original thought would have little place in my life.

In the fateful summer of 1914 she visited America. Unable to return to Germany, she taught for a time in a music school in Toronto. The following spring (1915) she started alone on a short vacation trip. Quite suddenly, while on the train, her weakened heart stopped beating.

CHAPTER TWO

WHAT CAUSES NATURAL SINGING?

SETTING UP THE RIGHT CONDITIONS

In a California canyon there is a garden, sprawling its delightful acre over irregularly sloping ground. On the uncultivated hill across the canyon laurels, oaks, red-trunked madroñas, and alders unite with a rampant growth of underbrush to delight the eye with every possible shade of green. Garden and hill are alike in that the same laws of nature manifest themselves in each. But the garden differs from the hill, for here man has deliberately set up favorable conditions through which those laws operate to even greater advantage than they could on the wild hill, where conditions are spontaneous and haphazard. It is the gardener's pleasurable business to find the soil best suited to each plant and shrub. Those that like sun and those that prefer shade are placed accordingly; those that need much water get it, and those that require little are protected from it. The gardener is merely *setting up conditions* most favorable to the well-being of the entire garden. But there his duty ends, and all that is left for him is to enjoy the resulting charm and beauty. How absurd it would be if the gardener felt it necessary to help the roses bloom or the sweetpeas blossom! And what a sorry mess he would make of it if he tried to do so! The garden would be ruined by his very conscientiousness.

Now let us imagine that the garden represents the student's voice and the gardener the student. He is the only person in the world able to prescribe conditions for that particular garden, and whether he realizes it or not, he is *always* setting up conditions there of some kind, either good or bad. The resulting beauty or lack of beauty in his singing is at once apparent to the listener—especially to the *outside* listener, to ears other than his own. If he is a relaxed, healthy person and if he is musical in the bargain, the chances are that the result— the sound of his voice—will be pleasing and full of charm, even thrilling if he happens to be in a buoyant mood. If he is stiff and locked, or weak, no matter how lovely the innate quality of his voice or how musical he may be, the result will be uncomfortable and to some degree ugly. The first instance resembles the glorious hill; the second case is like a desert waste that *could* "blossom like the rose" if only it were given the proper conditions. Even the lovely, natural un- trained voice could be improved if right conditions were established through which it could function, instead of this factor being left solely to chance. A grass fire would be far more apt to wreak disaster on the lovely hill than it would in the protected garden.

But many earnest people are not busying themselves particularly with consciously setting up right conditions for singing. Instead, they are most painstakingly and conscientiously opening up the buds and fussing with what is in reality the task of nature alone. They wish to produce "beautiful tones," and to this end are "focusing the voice," "moulding the lips," "lowering the larynx," "raising the soft palate," and in various ways *arranging the form* of the vocal instrument. They do not know that Nature and Nature alone is and should be the formative agent. Some of them are so determined to be thorough that they have invented mechanical devices for the sole purpose of "assisting" Mother Nature—the inference being that Mother Nature has grown into a helpless old person, incapable of attending to busi- ness. Shoehorn devices to hold the tongue in place, an upright stick designed to hold the jaws apart at the proper distance, weights to hang from the elbows, a belt of proper tension against which the diaphragm presses, thereby "strengthening" itself—these are some of the "aids" to "natural" singing! Needless to say, the results are artificial. For when man insists upon usurping Dame Nature's job, that lady, being the shyest thing in all the world, steps down and out immediately. And with her go true beauty, spontaneity, joy in singing or speaking, and the magic ability to move others, to carry a message through sincerity. Pandora's box has indeed been opened with a vengeance, and out fly all the hideous things that carry sorrow and disappointment and discomfort to earnest young people. But Hope remains, and it is never too late to put right conditions in the place of wrong ones. Nature will be as forgiving as she was shy, and will return if she is given only half a chance.

Now the "chance" Nature is longing for is what I have called "the setting up of right conditions." As singers, we recognize them through our senses of *feeling* and *hearing*. If you feel right and hear right you must sing "right." And presently you discover that, even as right results are invariably the consequence of right conditions, so every vocal failure can be traced unerringly to faulty conditions. With the needful conditions once established *and then continuously maintained,* the result is inevitable—a medium for dramatic expression that is at once beautiful and plastic, and capable of running the gamut of human emotion. If right conditions are established, *we* do not "do" the singing at all. Instead, *it gets done through us.*

But the worth or worthlessness of the foregoing statements can be proved only through personal experience. Let us take nothing at second hand. Let us instead throw tradition and traditional phrases to the four winds, for they are empty words unless our personal experience has first made them meaningful. The student's voice is entirely and most intimately his own. No one else can ever make use of it. He and he alone is on the inside track. His so-called "teachers" can never be more to him than "guides, philosophers, friends," forever on the outside. Let him teach himself to sing, then, in the spirit of an explorer setting out upon uncharted waters to discover new lands. Perhaps, like many discoverers, he will find something far more vast than the possibilities that first present themselves. If, like those explorers, he can maintain a faith in something yet unseen, faith in a Principle, an Idea, then nothing can hold back his reward.

No aviation pilot can fly higher or farther or more successfully than the mechanism of his plane permits. The student is both pilot and mechanic of his own voice, and if the mechanical side of his vocal training is accomplished with wisdom, persistence, and thoroughness, then nothing can hinder the artist within him from making a success of his work, the degree of his attainment being in direct proportion to his natural equipment.

CHAPTER THREE

FEELING AND HEARING

"If *feeling* and *hearing* are the only conditions for right singing, then *how* should I feel and *what* should I hear?" the student asks. As to the first half of this question, feel extremely *heavy* and at the same time feel extremely *full of life*. Words never have any meaning until they are translated into terms of personal experience. Try, then, the following experiment:

As you sit in your chair—a good straight dining-room chair is the right sort—concentrate on thinking a *heavy feeling* into every spot of your body. Your legs and arms weigh a ton each; your abdomen and your chest feel as though they were loaded with rocks; ear lobes, eyelids, fingers, have all been dipped into molten lead; even your teeth weigh a pound apiece; jaw, nose, cheeks, lips, tongue —there is not a single spot that is not intensely *weighty* and therefore *formless*. You feel like a colossally heavy jelly fish, for your backbone is no more. Let there be no limit to this feeling of great weight, and *never under any circumstances change this condition.* Instead, supplement it with another idea, again a condition of *feeling.* Decide to hoist this almost impossibly heavy load up out of the chair. When done with the right mental attitude this becomes a difficult problem, a slow and clumsy performance. You will find it easier to "get a purchase" under the "load" if you sit cornerwise on the chair, one foot at least 14 inches behind the other, toes pushing forcefully into the floor, while the heel of the forward foot likewise pushes down firmly. As you proceed to hoist the burden, be sure that the body

17

feels as though it were leaning somewhat backward rather than forward, as if it were hanging back, unwilling to be lifted. This is merely a *feeling* which insures your not bending and throwing the weight forward. What you are actually doing is maintaining the equilibrium of the body in a line perpendicular to the floor while feeling the effect entirely in the feet, legs, and buttocks. When you have reached a standing position you will find yourself *feeling* ready to sing, to dance, to do anything. Neither knees, abdomen, nor throat will feel stiff or clenched. Instead, you will be aware of a sensation of elasticity, vitality, boundless life. This is the power that lifted the burden up out of the chair, and unless you change the conditions by ceasing to feel heavy, you will be rewarded by a continuous sensation of buoyancy and levitation. Now this *power* is merely a process of nature, stretching through the heavy load and vitalizing every cell, taking the formless mass and forming it to best advantage.[1]

It may be accepted as axiomatic that "the more full of life one is, the better will be one's singing." If you will stop to think, you will see how very true it is that the heavier you can feel, the greater amount of life (power) it will take to move and lift the heavy load. *Power lifting relaxation* is the first requirement for right singing. Never lose that power! *Live with it,* regardless of whether or not you are singing. What you have discovered is not the principle that underlies singing alone, but the principle that is the foundation of *all physical action,* that of animals as well as of people. The moment of greatest relaxation is, potentially, the moment of greatest vitality, and from this paradox—this coinciding of apparent opposites—follow all inspiration and all work worthy of being called creative.

Perhaps you are puzzled by the statement that the feeling you experienced upon hoisting yourself up out of the chair was one of perfect readiness for physical accomplishment of any sort. Somehow, this new sensation does not in the least harmonize with the feelings

---

[1] Compare with paragraph commencing near bottom of page 8.

you remember from grammar school posture classes. Here is a true story that will illustrate this feeling better than pages of theorizing.

Once I spent an interesting morning visiting a class of six-year-old school children. At intervals the teacher would clap her hands saying, "Now children, we'll have some posture work. Now, feet together, weight on the balls of the feet, knees back, abdomen in, chest out, shoulders back, chin in, arms at your sides!" She would then demonstrate the desired position for the class. "Now, boys and girls, I am going to see how many of those little tummies are *in* and how many of those little chests are *out.*" Walking through the room, she would touch each small person as she passed. "Good for you, Jimmy! That tummy certainly is *in* and that chest is *out!* That's fine, Helen! A fine chest! No, Mary, dear, that isn't *quite* right. You see, dear, your tummy hangs and sticks out a little too far. Pull it in, dear! There, that's good! Then out with the little chest!" And so on down the line. I am afraid I was less interested in what the children were striving to do than in observing whether or not they maintained the "posture" that merited the teacher's praise. The moment the test had been satisfactorily passed, every little boy and girl *slumped,* unable to control all the different portions of the body any longer.

When, I wondered, will grown-ups realize that they are handing stones to children instead of bread when they give them a dozen different orders which the six-year-old mind is supposed to force upon the poor little six-year-old body—when they present them with a set of directions in place of a *principle,* a "what" for a "how?" If this prevailing reasoning had been really logical and correct, would not the oncoming generation be a glorious race of boys and girls with the grace and posture of ancient Greek youths? Should not freedom of bearing be the usual thing instead of the rare exception?

My thoughts were abruptly interrupted by the teacher who said, as she clapped her hands, "Children! Children! *Sit tall,* children! *Sit tall!*" And the little ones, all of whom had been lolling and sprawling over their desks, immediately "sat tall." At last a principle had been uttered, even though unconsciously. Not a dozen odd orders to be sent to as many different portions of the human frame, but *one principle,* one idea, one cause taking charge of each child's anatomy. *Power* was stretching through and lifting *relaxation.* "Sit tall!" The results were almost magical: the abdomens could not stick out, and the chests could not cave in; shoulders had no inclination to protrude, and heads were freely and beautifully poised at the top of elastic young spines. More than that, each child's body was working as a harmonious whole with all the unseen inner organs in place. Each child seemed able to maintain this simple condition at will.

So much, then, for *feeling,* the first of the two conditions necessary for right singing.

Now then, just what should you try to hear? As far as the correct singing of tones is concerned, only two things are important. They are pure vowels and purity of pitch. "But accuracy of pitch and proper vowel pronunciation are surely to be taken for granted!" the student will respond. "What about beauty of tone quality? What about resonance? What about breathing? What about tone color? What about enunciation and diction? What about flexibility? I'm sure it takes more than pure pitch and pure vowels to make beautiful singing!" These other things are *results,* not *causes.* If we attempt to *make* a beautiful resonant tone, we are no better than the stupid gardener who tries to *make* a beautiful blossom unfold, thus spoiling nature's work. When we are dealing with natural processes (and singing is only one of them) we should never forget that our business is to *attend to causes.* We are setting up the conditions *through* which nature creates beauty far lovelier than anything we could ever fashion. *Beauty always comes unsought.* It is a spontaneous thing. If we strive madly after it, it has a way of eluding us tragically.

An infant's first efforts at articulation can be of great value to us in our search after "pure" vowel sounds. Following the line of least resistance, his first *consciously repeated* vowel sound is apt to be "A" (as in mama or car). It is probably the easiest sound for him to utter, because he has done his crying on it since birth. As he develops, the other vowels soon follow, each one clear and single, unmixed and uncoupled with other vowel sounds. In these very first speech attempts, even an English or American baby uses no diphthongs.[1] He coos and babbles on clear, unchanging, unmixed, uncolored vowel sounds that seem to pass effortlessly through his vocal apparatus. As he grows older, he instinctively imitates the speech of those around him, and soon diphthongs and dulled vowel pronunciation supplant the bright, *carrying* sounds — the pure vowels — of his earlier infancy.

Now, the Italians, more than any other modern people, have preserved in their speech these primitive, fundamental, *pure* vowel sounds to which our ears have grown dull. A comparison between the Italian and English pronunciation of the five vowels A E I O U is illustrative:

Italian pronunciation as an American hears it:		English pronunciation as an Italian hears it:
AH	A	EI (a diphthong)
EH	E	I (a pure vowel)
EE	I	AI (a diphthong)
OH (spoken as in Irish dialect)	O	OU (a diphthong)
OO	U	IU (a "reversed diphthong")

(For a detailed explanation of the pronunciation of pure Italian vowels, see Chapter Six.)

It is plain that from the standpoint of its many diphthongs alone, English is far subtler and hence more difficult for preliminary voice

---

[1] Webster defines *diphthong* as: "A speech sound changing continuously from one vowel to another in the same syllable, as *ou* in *out* or *i* in *ice;* two vowel sounds joined in one syllable to form one speech sound." The Century Dictionary says a diphthong is "a coalition or union of two vowels pronounced in one syllable."

study than Italian. When the student has taught himself to hear the simple, separate, frank Italian vowels in all their clarity, it will interest him to learn that these pure vowels and their varied combinations are at the root of the vowel sounds of all languages, including English. The key that unlocks apparent difficulties facing him in the mastery of any language, then, is *true hearing and then true pronouncing of fundamental vowel sounds.* As a corollary to this discovery he will find that, for both speaking and singing, the same key unlocks the door to beauty of tone quality, resonance, and many other desired results.

Human beings are indeed creatures of habit and environment. If we Americans had been brought up in Italy, we might well take pronunciation of pure vowel sounds for granted, because speaking on pure vowels is the rule there and not the exception.[2] But we were born in the United States, where pure vowel sounds are seldom heard. It is imperative, therefore, that we train our ears to recognize the difference between pure vowel sounds and those that fall short of the mark. For only through pure vowel pronunciation can pure, beautiful, free tones be produced.

---

[2] The Italian singing masters of the 17th and 18th centuries are said to have instructed their pupils to "sing as you speak!"

CHAPTER FOUR

THE FOUNDATION OF GOOD ENGLISH DICTION

Spoken Italian is one of the simplest, hence closest to nature, of all our modern tongues. Its absolutely pure vowel sounds are thus fundamental to all speech and are the basis of all human utterance. If we listen carefully, we shall discover how these Italian vowels and their various combinations are at the root of the vowel sounds of *every* language. A careful examination of the table on page 21 will show their relation to the English vowels. The key that unlocks apparent difficulties facing us in the mastery of any language is *true hearing and then true pronouncing of fundamental vowel sounds.* For this reason we shall use the Italian rather than the English pronunciation of the five vowel sounds for our purpose.[1]

The five vowels are each the head of a separate "family," which we shall chart as follows:

THE VOWEL A AND ITS FAMILY

A   as in father
A2   as in ham
A3   as in all
A4   as in America

A — This sound (Italian A) is exactly half way between A2 and A3, and is often called "broad A" in English. Some people use this

---

[1] In the actual, non-phonetic spelling of English, these sounds are sometimes represented by other vowels. But we are dealing here with *pronunciation* — not spelling.

A (as in lard, calm, heart, etc.) in words such as hot, doll, God, log, etc.

A2 — The flat, ultra "bright" sounding member of this extensive family is the A in fat, sat, Sam, sack, flatter, track, clam, bangle, etc. In English this sound is never represented by any other letter.

A3 — as in tall, hall, etc. is exactly half way in sound between Italian A and Italian O.[2] Often called "short O," it is equally at home in the A family, and for practical purposes in singing I have placed it with the A's. The identical vowel sound occurs in such words as ought, naught, awful, augury, awl.

A4 — The U in up, the O in love, the E in the (before a word beginning with a consonant), the first A in alas — *all* have the same *sound*, and hence are the *same vowel*, no matter how absurdly varied their spelling. This odd vowel, so seldom found in other languages, is in English one of the most frequently met members of the A family.

The vowel E is the sole member of its family, and, despite varied spelling, presents no difficulties. Such words as edge, fair, penny, bent, head, said, wear, care, pare, pair, pear, etc. are common examples of this frequently encountered sound.

The Vowel I and its Family

I as in machine
Ĭ as in bitter

These vowel sounds are like twin brothers. They are easily recognized, no matter how varied their spelling: eat, greet, leak; it, grit, fit, lift.

The vowel O is one of the two remaining members of its family, because we have already disposed of "short O" by placing it in the A family as A3. We hear O in such words as go, know, dough, bureau; but in English we hear it *only* as a diphthong, OU, accom-

---

[2] Compare with the last group of examples above under A, which some people prefer to pronounce A3.

panied by the "vanishing vowel" U which closes it. It never occurs as a single (pure) vowel. Irish dialect, however, drops the U, leaving Italian O in full possession. Some Negro dialects show a preference for pure O. In speaking "stage English" (which should be our standard for speech), the voice rests in Italian O, and the vanishing U of the diphthong unites itself with the following cluster of consonants, as in the case of the first OU in the following:[3]

```
         I   hope  so
         A   ih0   ups0   u
```

The vowel Ö, while not exactly a "twin brother" to O, nevertheless definitely belongs in the O family.[4] It is the symbol for the vowel sound in such words as mirth, earth, thirty, curb, her, cur, heard, learn. It is always followed by the consonant R, which may be pronounced or not, according to preference and taste. Stage English usually drops the R following O:[5]

```
   I      heard     it      was     her      thirty-third
   A      ihÖ       rdĬ     tuA4    zhÖ      rthÖ  rtĬ  thÖ
                                            1          1
```

```
                     birthday.
                   rdbÖ  rthdE i
                         1
```

THE VOWEL U AND ITS FAMILY

U as in rude, brood, moon, etc.
Ŭ as in put, look, crook, push, etc.

---

[3] For a clarification of all of the following "blocked out" sentences, including the symbols under "th", see pages 27-29.

[4] See The Foundation of Good German Diction, page 35.

[5] In singing, if the R is used (this writer prefers it), it must *always* be rolled for all languages, though ever so slightly in singing English.

There are but two members of this family, and they present no complications:

```
Look    at      that    crude,   rude     person!
lŬ      kA2     tthA2   tkrU     drU      dpÖ rsA4 n
                  2
```

THE DIPHTHONGS

Besides the diphthong OU (already dealt with above under O) there are four others in English, as well as one "reversed diphthong." If we listen with care and concentration to these sounds as they drop into place, we begin to hear them as they really are. All difficulties disappear, and they become interesting instead of puzzling.

EI — The first letter of our English alphabet is in reality not one sound, but two. We find this very common sound in such words as hate, eight, came, bait, straight:

```
Today    eight    men     became    great.
tU dE    iE       itmE    nbI kE    imgrE it
```

AI — The ninth letter of the English alphabet[6] is, as we have seen, really two sounds. It is one of the most common diphthongs in our speech: Line, mighty, tight, I, lie, Guy, etc.

```
Tonight    Guy     might    fly.
tU nA      itgA    imA      itflA i
```

AU — We hear this diphthong in such words as house, how, ouch, now:

```
Now     how     hot     the       house    is.
nA      uhA     uhA     tthA4     ha       usĭz
                          2
```

---

[6] See The Foundation of Good German Diction, page 35, under AI-EI.

A3I — Another English diphthong frequently met with is the combination heard in such words as boy, joy, alloy, soil, noise, doily, etc.

```
    The      joyous,    noisy    boy.
    t̬hA4     jA3 iA4    snA3 izĭ  bA3 ĭ
    2
```

IU — The twenty-first letter of the English alphabet is what I term a "reversed diphthong." Unlike "regular" diphthongs, the short vowel of this pair *precedes* the long vowel. This combination is found in such words as lunar, Tuesday, few, new, knew, lieu, view, duke, etc.:

```
 Last      Tuesday    a    few    knew    it    was    true.
 1A2       sttiU zdE  iA4  fiU    niU     ĭ     t̬ŭA4  ztrU
```

If we listen with the utmost care, we shall discover that the English language lays itself out before us in the clearest and simplest way. The general pattern of any given sentence grows plain and reveals itself as a series of pure vowels, each one quite definite, each one belonging to one of the five vowel families. Clustered at the left side of these vowels are the consonants, the right side of every vowel remaining unattached to any consonant. In using the words "right" and "left," I am referring to the visual appearance of any sentence when it has been blocked out on paper.

When a vowel sound begins a sentence, that single pure vowel stands alone, no matter how many consonants may follow directly after it:

```
        almost      exhausted
        A3 lmO   ustE gzA3 stE d
```

If this first vowel is a diphthong, it still stands alone:

```
idle      words
A idA4  luÖ rdz
```

Likewise, when a word in the course of a sentence begins with a vowel sound that has been preceded by a syllable ending in a pure vowel, that beginning vowel stands alone:

```
Geneva     is   ·a     peaceful   city.
jE nI vA4  Ĭ    zA4    pI sfŬ     lsĬ tĬ
```

Any immediately succeeding vanishing vowel or consonant sounds cluster themselves with the *next* vowel sound, which, without exception, has nothing to do with any consonant sound following directly after it.

A few practical examples will clarify the foregoing explanation. But first let us establish a deciphering key:

In this key all superfluous symbols are discarded.

C   The letter (symbol) C does not appear, except in combination with H as in church, chair, etc. In words like center, scare, cat, cinder, etc. S and K take its place.

G   Only the hard G (as in grain, grave, gallop) is retained. Soft G (as in gentry, generous, religion, Geneva) is supplanted by J.

Q   The consonant Q is not used, K taking its place: quiet, quilt.

S   The sound of S in conversion, measure, pleasure is represented by ZH (the sound of J in French).

TH The two sounds of TH are written TH and TH: THank and
                                           1   2   1

THus.
2

W   The consonant W is used *only* in combination with H in such words as when, what, whether, wheat, where, etc. In words like we, want, watch, went, etc. the vowel U takes the place of W.

X   This consonant is unnecessary, Z taking its place in words like xylophone, Xanthippe, etc. In words like extract and fix, KS takes the place of X.

Y   The vowel Y is discarded except when it precedes a vowel (as in yacht, yet, ye, yeast, yearn, yoke, you, etc.); otherwise its place is filled by i: bóy, Guy, hay, play, nay.

Note. When two consonants combine to make one sound, they are joined thus:

```
      th   th   wh   ch   sh   ng
      1    2
```

```
George Arliss said:   "By      good      diction       I
                       bA      igŬ      ddĬ kṣhA4 n     A

   mean      the    speaking      of     words    correctly
   imI     nthA4    spI kĬ       ng̑A4    vuö     rdzkA3 rE ktlĬ
            2


and      easily."
A2    ndI  zĬ  lĬ


Epictetus said:   "No      great      thing      is
                   n0      ugrE      itṭhĬ      ng̑Ĭ

   created      suddenly,     any      more      than      a
   zkrI E itE   dsA4 dE nlĬ   E nĬ     mA3     rṭhA2     nA4
                                               2

bunch      of     grapes      or      a      fig.      If      you
bA4     ṇchA4    vgrE      ipsA3    rA4    fĬ g       Ĭ      fiU
```

```
tell     me     that     you     desire     a     fig,     I
tE     lmI     thA2     tiU     dĬ zA     irA4     fĬ g     A
                2
```

```
answer     you     that     there     must     be
iA2 nsÖ     riU     thA2     tthE     rmA4     stbI
                     2        2
```

```
time.     Let     it     first     blossom,     then
tA im     lE     tĬ     tfÖ     rstblA sA4m     thE
                                                 2
```

```
bear     fruit,     then     ripen."
nbE     rfrU t     thE     nrA ipA4n
                   2
```

```
Actors     and     actresses     ought     to
A2 ktA3     rzA2     ndA2 ktrE sE     zA3     ttU
```

```
articulate     distinctly.
A rtĬ kiU lE     itdĬ stĬ ñgktlI.
```

```
Michelangelo said:     "What     one     takes     the
                       whA4     tuA4     ntE     iksthA4
                                                 2
```

```
greatest     pains     to     do     should     look     as
grE itE     stpE     inztU     dU     shŬ     dlŬ     kA2
```

```
if     it     had     been     thrown     off     quickly,
zĬ     fĬ     thA2     dbI     nthr0     unA3     fkuĬ klĬ
```

```
almost     without     effort -- nay -- in     despite
A3 lm0     ustuĬ thA     utE fA3 rt     nE i     Ĭ     ndĬ spA·
             2
```

```
 of      the      truth,     as      though     it      cost
itA4    vthA4     trU th     A2      ztho       uĬ      tkA3
         2            1                 2


 one     no      trouble.    The     great      precept
stuA4    nnO     utrA4 bA4 l thA4    grE        itprI sE
                                2


 is:     'Take     infinite     pains,     and      make
ptĬ z     tE      ikĬ nfĬ nĬ    tpE inz     A2      ndmE


 something      that      looks      effortless!'"
iksA4 mthI     ̂ngthA2     tlŬ        ksE fA3 rtlE s
        1          2



Leisure   and    pleasure    without    any      measure
1E zhÖ    rA2   ndplE zhÖ    ruĬ thA   utE nĬ    mE zhÖ r
                                 2
```

LOVE HAS EYES

Words by Charles Dibdin   Music by Henry Rowley Bishop

```
Love's      blind      they      say,     0      never,     nay,
1A4        vzblA      indthE     isE i    0      unE vA4    rnE i
                         2


Can      words     love's      grace      impart?
kA2      nuÖ      rdzlA4       vzgrE      isĬ mpA rt
          A4


The      fancy     weak      the      tongue      may      speak,
thA      fA nsĬ    uI k      thA4     tA4        ̂ngmE     ispI k
 2                            2
```

```
But      eyes     alone     the      heart.
bA4      tA       izA4 10   unthA4   hA rt
                              ‿
                              2


In    one     soft      look      what      language      lies,
Ĭ     nuA4    nsA3      ftlU      kwhA4     tlA2 ñgguE     jlA iz
                                    ‿


0     yes,    believe   me,       love      has      eyes --
0     uyE s   bĬ lI     vmI       lA4       vhA2     zA iz


          0,       Love     has      eyes!
          0        ulA4     vhA2     zA iz


Love's      winged      they      cry,     0      never,     I
lA4         vzuĬ        ñgdthE     ikrA i   0      unE vA4 r  A
                          ‿
                          2


No      pinions     have      to      soar!
n0      upĬ nyA4    nzhA2     vtU     sA3 r


Deceivers     rove      but      never     love,
dĬ sI vA4     rzr0 uv   bA4      tnE vA4   rlA4 v


Attached,          he       roves     no       more!
A2tA2       çht    hI       r0        uvzn0    umA3 r


Can     he      have      wings ‿   who      never     flies!
kA2     nhI     hA2       vuĬ       ñgzhU    nE vA4    rflA   iz


And   yet,    believe    me,     Love has   eyes - - -
A2    ndiE    tbĬlI      vmI     lA4  vhA2   za iz


          --  0 love has etc.
```

CHAPTER FIVE

THE FOUNDATION OF GOOD GERMAN DICTION

In German we find the vowel sounds we already know in English (see Chapter Four, The Foundation of Good English Diction) together with several new ones that do not exist in our language.

In German, as in English, there are the same four members of the A family:

A as in Vater, Magd, lachen

A2 as in flattern, Fabrik

A3 as in Tochter, horch, doch, Otto[1] (first syllable); and in the stressed (first) part of the diphthongs in aus, auf, Haus and beugen, Träume.

A4 as in Vater, Mutter, Butter, Vetter, etc. (last syllables). In German the final syllable of all words ending in ER is unaccented, and the vowel therein is pronounced A4. In speech, but usually not in singing, the final R is generally omitted. This vowel, A4, so common in English,

---

[1] The sound of Ŏ (short O) before a doubled consonant and before the consonant R is, in all languages, the sound of A3 (as in all, maul, call). This is also true in German when O is followed by ch. See The Foundation of Good English Diction, page 24. In German this sound (A3) is never represented by the symbol A except in the diphthong AU as in Haus, rauschen, etc. (See German diphthongs, page 36.) In dealing with German diction, we shall continue to place the *sound* of short O in the A family as A3, despite its spelling.

is never found otherwise in German. English-speaking persons are apt to pronounce the vowel E in the final syllable of such words as Liebe, gute, fechten, machen, etc. as though it were A4. This mispronunciation is offensive to German ears, and should be changed to Ö. (See page 35.)

In German we find three members in the E family:

E   as in es, des, der, letzt, Elbe (first syllable)

É   as in dem, den, gehen, sehen (first syllables). This sound, É, is exactly half way between that of Italian E and Italian I — as though one spoke these two vowels at one and the same time. It is a single, very intense sound, a pure vowel, and should never degenerate into the diphthong EI as in May, Amy, hay, crave. It always occurs in an accented syllable.

Ä   as in quälen, ärgern, Mädchen. Ä is exactly half way between A2 and E. It is not difficult to pronounce this rather subtle vowel if one merely speaks a pure Italian E *through an A mouth.*

The I family is just as we found it in English, except for one strange and important addition — Ü. In pronouncing this vowel, one merely speaks pure I *through U lips.* Though this may be a new sound to most American ears, it is neither difficult nor confusing. The four members of the I family are:

I   as in mir, dir, Liter

Ĭ   as in bis, mich, singen

Ü̱   as in müde, lügen

Ü̆   as in küssen, schütteln, Glück. The sound of Ü̆ occurs before a doubled consonant and before CK. The correct pronunciation is attained when one speaks Ĭ *through U lips.*

Since we have already placed short Ŏ in the A family as A3,[2]
the two remaining members of the O family are:

O as in Vogel, schon, Mond. The German O is one pure
sound, and must not be pronounced like our English O,
a diphthong OU. It sounds darker than Italian O, and is
attained when one pronounces Italian U and Italian O
at the same time.

Ö as in schön, mögen, Löwe. The sound of Ö is not difficult for English-speaking people to acquire. It is the exact
vowel sound in the English word HER, with the consonants H and R removed. Actually, it is a combination
of the Italian vowels E and O, spoken simultaneously.
See page 33, under A4; also The Foundation of Good
English Diction, page 25, under Ö.

The U family is simple, and exactly as we found it in English:

U as in Ruh, Mut, Kuh

Ŭ as in und, uns, Wunder

THE GERMAN DIPHTHONGS

The following English diphthongs do not exist in German:

OU as in own, tone, loan.

EI as in aim, shame, lay.

A3I as in boy, foil, noise. (Compare with EU and ÄU below.)

IU (the inverted diphthong) as in use, new, few.

The Germans have two ways of writing the sound of the ninth
letter in our English alphabet (i):

AI as in Mai, Hain, Mainz

EI as in mein, dein, einst

---

[2] See The Foundation of Good English Diction, page 24.

In singing one pronounces this diphthong A2E rather than AI; the latter sound is generally used in spoken German as in spoken English.

Our diphthong AU (as in now, house, etc.) is nearly the same in German. The difference is in the principal vowel, A, which the Germans pronounce very darkly, A3:

rauschen	auf	Auge	Frau	kaum
rA3 ushÖ n	A3 uf	A3 ugÖ	frA3 u	ka3 um

The Germans have two ways of writing another diphthong, one that does not exist in English. It is pronounced A3O:

ÄU as in	Bäume	Tannhäuser
	bA3 ömÖ	tA nnhA3 ösA4 r

EU as in	Freund	leuchtend	Deutsch
	frA3 önd	1A3 öchtE nd	dA3 öch

Americans are apt to confuse this diphthong with our own A3I, as in joy (see above), but German ears hear a decided difference between our incorrect I and their Ö at the close of this diphthong.

The following English consonant sounds do not exist in German:
  TH as in this, think, that
  WH as in which, what, when
  J   as in judge, gentle, judicious
  S   (Pronounced ZH) as in treasure, seizure, pleasure

The consonant Q is found written *only* in combination with the vowel U, as in the case of English. In German QU is pronounced KV:

qualen	quälen	quellen	quillen	quollen
kvA 1Ö n	kvÄ 1Ö n	kvE 11Ö n	kvĬ 11Ö n	kvA3 11Ö n

The letter N before K in such words as danke, dunkel, Onkel, denken is pronounced NG, as it is in our English words think, thank, drink, honk.

In singing, the sound of S (as in Musik, Eisen, Seufzer) should never be softened into Z as in the English word "dizzy." Instead, it inclines more towards the sound of S in the English words set, such, with just a tinge of the S in music, physic, etc.

S before T or P when beginning a word is always pronounced S̰H:

stehen	Stein	Stimme	sparen	Spohr	Spur
s̰htE Ö n	s̰htA2 en	s̰htĬ mmŌ	s̰hpA rö n	s̰hpA3 r	s̰hpU r

Z is never pronounced as it is in English (maze, fuzz, jazz). In German this letter represents two united sounds, TS:

Mainz	zu	Mozart
mA2 en̰ts	t̰sU	mO t̰sA rt

C̰H. The sound of this combination of letters is different from any we have in English, though Scotch dialect has similar sounds, as in "loch" for lake. It occurs when one lets the breath pass between the tongue and the palate when they are almost touching. When preceded by the vowel sounds A, A3, U or Ŭ, the *back* of the tongue and the soft palate are involved:

ach	doch	Bruch	suchen	Buch
A c̰h	dA3 c̰h	brŬ c̰h	sU c̰hö n	bUc̰h

When preceded by consonant sounds or by the vowel sounds I, Ĭ,

A2E, A3Ö, E, Ö, the *middle* of the tongue and the *hard* palate are involved:

```
welch      riechen    ich      bleich    euch     sechs
vE lch     rI chö n   Ï ch     blA2 ech  A3 öch   sE chs
```

```
           Köchin     Mädchen
           kö chI n   mÄ dchö n
```

The suffix IG is pronounced in spoken German as though it were spelled "ich":

```
    König      gnädig      selig      hungrig
    kö nÏ ch   gnÄ dÏ ch   sE lÏ ch   hÜ nggrÏ ch
```

This it not always the case in singing, however. It is a matter of taste as to whether one pronounces this suffix "ich," or "ig" as in the English word fig. In serious, dignified phrases such as those found in much of Richard Wagner's music, the hard ending is preferred. In less impressive, less formal music and in all folksongs the soft ending is used.

When S is placed before CH, the result is merely SH:

```
    Schein     zwischen    lauschen
    shA2 en    tsvÏ shö n  1A3 ushö n
```

The consonant W is pronounced V:

```
    wenn      Wien     Wein      welche
    vE nn     vI n     vA2 en    vE lch Ö
```

V is pronounced F:

Vater	Vetter	von
fA tA4 r	fE ttA4 r	fA3 n

J is considered a consonant, and is usually found preceding a vowel:[1]

jeder	jene	jung	Jena	ja
yÉ dA4 r	yÉ nö	yŬ n͡g	yÉ nA	yA

The final D in many, but not all, words is pronounced T:

Kind	und	Land	Feind	Freund	Wund
kĬ nt	Ŭ nt	1A nt	fA2 end	frA3 önd	vŬ nd

The final B in some, but not all, words is pronounced P:

ab	ob
A p	0 b

Doubled consonants, which are treated negligibly in English, must be carefully considered in German. If one *rests* for a fraction of time in the *form*[2] of a single consonant, it becomes a doubled consonant. In the basic practicing of a song, however, it is wise to treat doubled consonants as though they were single, until a sure *legato* has been established.

All other German consonants are pronounced exactly as they are

---

[1] Compare with last paragraph (Y), page 29.

[2] By "form" is meant the natural position of throat and mouth compelled by the utterance of a single consonant.

in English. (See Chapter IV, The Foundation of Good English Diction, page 28.)

It is important for the singing student to *hear* the words of a given song pronounced by an educated German with a good accent. "Bühnen Deutsch," like "stage English," is the standard of good speech. This chapter will, I hope, simplify the pronunciation problems that may confront the student, so that he will become less dependent upon such help.

Following is a short German song blocked out for the use of the student in studying German diction.

GUTE NACHT

Joseph von Eichendorff   Robert Franz, Op. 5, No. 7

```
Die     Höh'n    und     Wälder    schon    steigen
dI      hÖ       nŬ      ntvÄ 1dA4  rṣhO     nṣhtA2 egÖ n

immer      tiefer    in's      Abendgold;
Ĭ mmA4     rtI fA4    rĬ       nsA bÖ ntgA3 lt

ein     Vöglein    fragt     in    den    Zweigen
A2      enfÖ glA2   enfrA     ktĬ   ndÉ    ntsvA2 egÖ n

ob      es    Liebchen     grüssen     sollt'?
O       bE    slI bçhÖ      ngrÜ ssÖ    nsA3 llt

O       Vöglein,    du       hast    dich      betrogen;
O       fÖ glA2     endU     hA      stdĬ      çhbE trO gÖ n

sie     wohnet    nicht     mehr     im     Thal!
sI      vO nE     tnĬ       çhtmE    rĬ     mtA l

schwing'    auf      dich     zum      Himmelsbogen;
shvĬ        n͡gA3     ufdĬ     çhtsŬ    mhĬ mmE 1sbO gÖ n

grüss'    sie     droben . . . . . zum      letztenmal!
grÜ       szI     drO bÖ n . . . . . tsŬ    mlE tztÖ nmA l
```

CHAPTER SIX

THE FOUNDATION OF GOOD ITALIAN DICTION

In Italian we find the first three members of the A family already encountered in English:[1]

```
A  as in  calma     natura     manca
          kA lmA     nA tU rA   mA nkA
```

```
A2 as in  abbasso       abbattuto       vacca
          A2 bbA2 ss0   A2 bbA2 ttU t0  vA2 kkA
```

A2 is always followed by a doubled consonant.

```
A3 as in  nostri     ogni     donna       constanti
          nA3 strI   A3 nyI   dA3 nnA     kA3nstA ntI
```

```
          stagion        tortorella       vorrei       amor
          stA jA3 n      tA3 rtA3 rE llA  vA3 rrE i    A mA3 r
```

A3 is always followed by a doubled consonant, by two differing consonants, or by the single consonant R. Although this sound is always symbolized in Italian by Ŏ ("short O") we place it in the A family for all languages.[2]

---

[1] See The Foundation of Good English Diction, page 23.
[2] See The Foundation of Good English Diction, A3.

41

The E family consists of three members:[3]

```
E as in che     vede    per    grembo    vivere
        kE      vE dE   pE r   grE mb0   vI vE rE

E as in ebete      leva       lettiera      gelo
        É bE tE   lÉ vA      lE ttyÉ rA    jÉ 10

        gemere
        jÉ mE rE
```

The pronunciation É occurs only in stressed syllables. It is slightly less intense in Italian than it is in German, leaning a trifle *less* towards I than in German.

```
E as in bello     gemma     belta     venti
        bÄ 110    jÄ mmA    bÄ 1tA    vÄ ntI

        stretto
        strÄ tt0
```

The symbol Ä stands for the same pure vowel sound as it does in German. It occurs rather infrequently in Italian and is usually (though not always) found before doubled consonants, or two differing consonants.

In Italian there is but one member in the I family:

```
I as in  il     in    moti     si
         I 1   I n   m0 tI     sI
```

---

[3] Compare the Italian E family with the German in The Foundation of Good German Diction, page 34.

```
      innocente        mille        città
      I nnO chE ntE    mI llE       chI ttA

      dissentire
      dI ssE ntI rE
```

Since we have already placed Ŏ in the A family as A3,[4] there remains but one member in the O family:

```
O as in  sol      con      non      suo      mio
         sO l      kO n     nO n     sUO      mIO

         lido     solo
         lI dO    sO lO
```

In Italian there is but one member in the U family. This is the same sound as in our English word "prune":

```
U as in  usato      pur     un      tutta     sua
         U sA tO    pU r     U n     tU ttA    sUA
```

In Italian there are no diphthongs represented by a single vowel as in the English words

```
      hate     fine     so     cute
      hE it    fA in    sO u   kiU t
```

Italians spell out these sounds by means of two vowels:

```
      vorrei        mai      diurno     più
      vA3 rrE i     mA i     dy U rnO   pyU
```

---

[4] See The Foundation of Good English Diction, page 24. Also A3, page 41 of this chapter.

The Italian Consonants

The following English consonant sounds do not occur in Italian:
TH   as in think, this, etc.
WH   as in what, when, etc.
S   as in treasure, pleasure, etc.

As in English, Q is invariably followed by the vowel U:

```
questa      quella      quarto      quasi
kuE stA     kuE llA     kuA rto     kuA sI
```

The sound of S should never be softened into Z, as in the English word "jazz." Instead, it is more like the S in psalm, set, seem, so, soon.

The sound of CH in chest, cheese, etc., is conveyed in Italian by C before E and I:

```
ceffo           cima
chE ffO         chI mA
```

If the CH sound is followed by A, O, or U, a practically inaudible I is placed between C and the adjacent vowel:

```
ciano       ciotola     ciuco
chA nO      chO tO lA   chU kO
```

Without the I these words would be pronounced:

```
cano        cotola      cuco
kA nO       kO tO lA    kU kO
```

The sound of S̪H in shelter, shimmer, etc. is symbolized in Italian by SC when it stands before E and I:

```
        scena       scintilla
        s̪hÉ nA      s̪hI ntĬ 11A
```

If the SH sound is followed by A, O, or U, a practically silent I is placed between C and the adjacent vowel:

```
        sciarpa     sciolo      sciupare
        s̪hA rpA     s̪h0 10      s̪hU pA rE
```

Without the I, these words would be pronounced:

```
        scarpa      scolo     scupare
        skA rpA     sk0 10    skU pA rE
```

The letter J is not found in the Italian alphabet, but its sound is expressed by placing G before E and I:

```
        gemma       giro
        jE mmA      jI r0
```

When the J sound is followed by A, O, or U, a practically inaudible I is placed between G and the following vowel:

```
    gia     giara     giocoso     giungere
    jA      jA rA     j0 k0 s0    jU njE rE
```

Without the I these words would be pronounced:

```
    ga      gara     gocoso      gungere
    gA      gA rA    g0 k0 s0    gU njE rE
```

Although the letter H is sometimes used in Italian, it is never pronounced:

ah	ha	ho	ohi
A	A	O	OI

K is never used as a symbol, C and CH expressing its sound:

calma	cheto	china	compra	cura
kA lmA	kE tO	kI nA	kO mprA	kU rA

W, X, and Y are not in the Italian alphabet.

The letter Z symbolizes in Italian the sound of TS, just as it does in German:[5]

grazia	zaffiro	zeppa	zia	zolfo	zufolo
grA tsI	A tsA2 ffI rO	tsE ppA	tsI A	tsA3 lfO	tsU fO lO

The blocked-out sounds "lyI" and "ny" seem strange to our ears:

gli	Gigli	compagno	bisogno	prugna
lyI	jI lyI	kO mpA nyO	bI sO nyO	prU nyA

Doubled consonants, often treated carelessly in English, must be most carefully considered in Italian.[6] If one rests for a fraction of time in the *form* of a single consonant, it becomes a doubled consonant.[7]

---

[5] See The Foundation of Good German Diction, page 37.
[6] Ignoring Italian doubled consonants is a common fault of foreigners. To Italian ears this is unpardonable!
[7] See The Foundation of Good German Diction, page 39.

The consonants B D F L M N P R S T V are pronounced exactly as in English.[8]

This chapter will, I hope, help you acquire a fine Italian accent in speaking and singing. However, it is of paramount importance to listen to the speech of a cultivated Italian, if only to corroborate what has here been set forth.

A short song, *Sebben crudele*, by Antonio Caldara (1670-1736) is presented as an example of blocking out for singing in Italian:

SEBBEN CRUDELE

Antonio Caldara

```
Sebben,     crudele,    mi    fai     languir,
sE bbE    nkrU dE lE   mI    fA I    lA nguI r


sempre    fedele      ti    voglio    amar
sE mprE  fE dE lE     tI    vO lyO    A mA r


Con    la    lunghezza    del     mio    servir
kO    nlA   lU ngE tsA    dE    lmI O    sE rvI r


la    tua    fierezza    sapro     stancar.
lA    tUA    fyE rE tsA  sA prO   stA nkA r
```

---

[8] See The Foundation of Good English Diction, page 128.

CHAPTER SEVEN

THE FOUNDATION OF GOOD
FRENCH DICTION

The pure basic Italian vowel sounds, though often subtly shaded, manifest themselves clearly in French, albeit often through spelling that seems strange and illogical to foreigners.

In French, as in English and German, we find the same four members of the A family:

```
A   as in âme     hélas     pas
         A m      É lA s     pA


A2 as in charme    reçoit    sa     la     après.
         shA2 rm   rö suA2   sA2    1A2    A2 prÁ
            ⌣ 1           1       1      1      1


         jamais
         zhA2 mÄ
            ⌣ 1
```

Cultured French somewhat tempers the otherwise too flat sound of A2 with that of A1.

```
A3 as in  joli     forme     soleil
          zhA3 1I  fA3 rm    sA3 1E y
             ⌣
```

In French spelling the sound of A3 is always represented by O.

```
A4 as in comme     somme      comment     hommes
       kA4 m       sA4 m      kA4 mA      A4 m
                                 n
```

In French spelling the sound of A4 is always represented by O.

French speech has one characteristic peculiarly its own — the nasal vowel sounds. A true French nasal sound occurs when the soft palate is absolutely relaxed, thereby leaving open the passage from nose to throat.

Curiously enough, these nasal sounds are confined entirely to *one* of the five vowel families — the A family — regardless of how they are spelled.

```
A   spoken nasally becomes A as in an   en   ent   enfant
                           n        A    A    A     A fA
                                    n    n    n     n  n

A2 spoken nasally becomes A2 as in ain   fin   bien
                          n        A2    fA2   byA2
                                   n     n     n

                                   rien   plain
                                   ryA2   plA2
                                   n      n
```

(Nasal A2 is rather flat and untempered.)

```
A3 spoken nasally becomes A3 as in on   son   confond
                          n        A3   sA3   kA3 fA3
                                   n    n     n   n
                                              nombre
                                              nA3 br
                                              n
```

(In French spelling this sound is always represented by *on* or *om.*)

```
A4 spoken nasally becomes A4 as in un   Verdun   brun
               n              A4  vE rdA4 brA4
                              n       n    n
                                          humble
                                          A4 bl
```

(This vowel sound — the U in our English word "up," spoken nasally — is somewhat influenced by Ö, a good illustration of the subtlety of French speech.)

The French E family is practically like the German, although the spelling of two of its members is multiform:

```
E as in   ette      ternir      fermer
          E t       tE rnI r    fE rmÉ

É as in   étang     trouver     référer
          É tA      trU vÉ      rÉ fÉ rÉ
          n
```

```
Ä as heard in   mais    des plaine   aimer   peine
                mÄ      dÄ  plÄ n     Ä mÉ    pÄ n

                bête    mère  elle
                bÄ t    mÄ r  Ä l
```

(For use in blocking out, the symbol Ä is borrowed from the German, because it represents one definite sound or

pronunciation. See The Foundation of Good German
Diction, page 34.

In the I family in French, I (as in fit, English; frisch, German)
does not exist. This leaves but two members of the I family in use:

```
I as in   suis      si      il      soupire      dire
          süI       sI      I l     sU pI r      dI r

Ü as in   pur       plus    refuser     fût
          pÜ r      plÜ     rÖ fÜ zÉ    fÜ
```

In French spelling this sound is always represented by
U. The symbol Ü is borrowed from the German because
it represents a definite pronunciation. See The Foundation
of Good German Diction, page 34.

There are two members in the French O family (see A3, page
41; also The Foundation of Good English Diction, page 24:)

```
0 as in   eau       au      tôt     mot
          0         0       t0      m0

Ö as in   je        se      leva    le      que     feu
          zhÖ       sÖ      lÖ vA   lÖ      kÖ      fÖ

          deux      petit
          dÖ        pÖ tI
```

In singing and in poetry the final E is usually pronounced, though
rather casually:

```
grande      image        `âme        mine
grA dÖ      I mA2 zhÖ     A mÖ        mI nÖ
  n           l
```

(For blocking-out purposes the German symbol Ö is used because it represents a definite pronunciation. See The Foundation of Good German Diction, page 35.)

When followed (in the same syllable) by a consonant, the pronunciation of Ö is usually altered a trifle by hanging the mouth into a slight smile. This more open sound is symbolized by O as in:

```
seul   coeur   fleur   couleur   peur   neuf   jeune   peuple
sO̤ l   kö̤ r    flö̤ r   kU lö̤ r    pö̤ r   nö̤ f   zhö̤ n   pö̤ pl
   <      <        <          <       <      <       <       <
```

There is but one member in the French U family, and it is always spelled with the two letters OU:

```
U as in   brouée    coup    sous    mouton
          brU É     kU      sU      mU tA3
                                       n
```

Ŭ as in the English words put, full, pull, does not exist in French.

Diphthongs as we know them in English do not exist in French.

The following consonant sounds are unknown in French:
TH   as in this, think, that
WH   as in which, what, when
J   as in gentle, judge, jury

The sound of H (as in house) is rarely heard in French.

The French consonants are pronounced more or less as in English with the following exception:

J is always pronounced like the sound of S in our English words lesion, treasure, version, and is symbolized by ZH. See The Foundation of Good English Diction, page 28.

The French doubled consonants, as in English (but not as in German and Italian), are not overly stressed.

In endeavoring to master French, perhaps one of the most difficult sounds for Americans is that found in such words as

```
        encore          sombre
        A kA3  r        sA3 br
        n               n
```

We are apt to pronounce them

```
        encore          sombre
        A ngKA3  r      sA3 mbr
        n               n
```

forgetting that the N and M have *already* been spoken when the vowel preceding them has been uttered *nasally*.

Although French is admittedly the subtlest of all languages, it is helpful to realize that *any sound in any language can be blocked out,* thus minimizing the difficulties that beset one in speaking or singing in a foreign tongue. In dealing with French in particular, it is wise if not necessary to hear the words of a given song spoken by a Parisian. "Parisian French" is conceded to be the standard.

Appended is a blocked out example of a simple French song.

CHANTONS LES AMOURS DE JEAN

[from *Bergerettes of the Eighteenth Century.*]

```
1.  Chantons,    chantons    les    amours    de
    shA tA3      shA tA3     lE     zA2 mU     rdö
      n   n        n   n            l

                                    Jeanne,
                                    zhA2 nö
                                        l
```

```
Chantons,       chantons     les     amours      de      Jean.
shA tA3         shA tA3      lE      zA2 mU      rdÖ     zhA
   n  n            r  n               l                    n
```

```
         Rien      n'est    si     charmant     que     Jeanne,
         ryA2      nE       sI     shA2 rmA     kÖ      zhA2 nÖ
           n                         l   n                   l
```

```
            Rien     plus    aimable        que     Jean.
            ryA2     plÜ     zÄ mA2 blÖ     kÖ      zhA
              n                 l                     n
```

```
   Jean      aime      Jeanne,      Jeanne      aime      Jean,
   zhA       nÄ mÖ     zhA2 nÖ      zhA2        nÄ m0     zhA
     n                      l          l                   n
```

```
Jean      aime      Jeanne,      Jeanne      aime      joli
zhA       nÄ mÖ     zhA2 nÖ      zhA2        nÄ mÖ     zhA3lI
  n                      l          l
```

```
                                                        Jean.
                                                        zhA
                                                          n
```

```
2.  Dans      une      simple      cabane,
    dA        zÜ nÖ    sA2 plÖ     kA2 bA2 nÖ
      n                   n           l   l
```

```
Comme      en      un      palais,      tout      d'or
kA4        mA      nA4     pA2 lÄ       tU        dA3
             n       n       l
```

```
                                           brillant,
                                           rbrI yA
                                                 n
```

```
         Jean      reçoit     l'amour     de      Jeanne,
         zhA       rÖ suA2    lA2 mU      rdÖ     zhA2 nÖ
           n            l        l                     l
```

```
Et      Jeanne    celui    de     Jean.
É       zhA2 nÖ   sÖ lüI   dÖ     zhA
          ‿l                        ‿n
```

Jean aime Jeanne etc.

```
3.  Si    l'amour    de      Jeanne    est     grande,
    sI     1A2 mU    rdÖ     zhA2      nE      grA dÖ
             l                 ‿l                 n
```

```
Non     moins     grande    est     l'amitié    de
nA3     muA2      grA       dE      1A2 mI tyÉ   dÖ
 n       n         n                  l
```

```
                                                Jean.
                                                zhA
                                                  ‿n
```

```
Ce      que      l'un     des     deux    demande
sÖ      kÖ       1A4      dE      dÖ      dÖ mA dÖ
                   n                         n
```

```
L'autre         aussitôt    y     consent.
10              trO sI tO    I     kA3 sA
                                     n    n
```

Jean aime Jeanne etc.

CHAPTER EIGHT

MOTION — "THE ESCALATOR"

From many years of teaching I have concluded that, broadly speaking, faulty voices divide into those that are breathy and mushy, and those that are harsh and hard.

Breathy voices are inoffensive and are often rather pleasing in quality, though not powerful. Hard voices are shrill in quality, and very powerful.

Breathy voices have little resonance and do not carry. "Only a parlor voice," we say. Hard voices carry all too well, and they seem overpowering in an ordinary room. "I wish I could hear that voice in a big hall!" we say.

The diction of a singer with a breathy voice is fairly easy to understand. The diction of a singer with a hard voice is never easily understood. Nevertheless, these hard, piercing, dry voices contain an important and necessary factor of good singing — *resonance*. But it is, so to speak, resonance "gone haywire." Why? Because such voices lack living, moving breath.

The ancient Italian masters left a few simple statements on singing. One important command was, "Sing on the breath!" Now, as we have just seen, a breathy voice is merely singing on the breath gone haywire, because such a voice is almost devoid of resonance. If the breathy singers could only get resonance and if the shrill singers could only get some breath into their voices from top to bottom, then breath and resonance would *automatically* come into balance and

56

act as checks on each other. There would be neither hard, static quality nor leakage of breath. In place of these faults, beautiful, carrying, *moving* voices would result. *Motion,* the charming, vital thing in singing, is the outcome, then, of breath plus resonance. *Both elements* must be in every tone of a good voice. The more perfect the balance between them, throughout the entire range, the more pleasing a voice becomes. A *way of singing* is thus established, and it is this *way* that we recognize as "good singing."

A "moving voice" (that is to say, one that stirs the emotions of the listener) is one that is literally *in motion* (that is to say, a voice moving through a non-static body). Our problem is to find the reason for this motion. What is the *principle* behind it?

We have all known young, untrained voices that possessed this quality. In trying to describe them, people say, "His voice just *rolls* out!" or "Her voice seems to *float!*" Then somehow, after a course of singing lessons, the charm is gone. "I used to like her voice before she had so much training," we say. "Now it sounds overtrained and has lost all its sweetness." That training should spoil rather than improve a lovely natural voice seems illogical. If our young friend once possessed the power to move people by her voice, a wise teacher should have developed this gift by explaining what caused it. Instead, because she cannot associate the charming, moving *effect* with a dependable *cause,* the talented young singer is too apt to take this beguiling quality of youth — this *motion* — for granted. In the course of time she loses it.

It is apparent enough that clear diction is an indispensable part of an emotionally moving voice, and that such a voice is produced only by an instrument that is itself vital and moving. To become such an instrument, the body must be and remain unclutched — *completely relaxed without any reservation whatever.* This idea is the *first link* in a logical chain of *cause and effect* that controls *feeling.* The second link is the idea of *vitality,* which catches this relaxed instrument and keeps it from falling to the ground. "The moment of greatest relaxation *is* the moment of greatest vitality." The heavier I feel, the more power is instantly generated to lift the great weight.

Now, having set up this condition of *power working through relaxation,* we have returned, physically, to the state of early childhood. As a result, the functions of breathing and utterance (laughter, weeping, and all other human sounds, intelligible and otherwise) come naturally and efficiently because they are *ordered, but not managed, by the individual.* A baby's earliest attempts at speech consist chiefly of vowel sounds. These are clear and unmixed, similar to Italian, Hawaiian, and other languages built principally on vowel sounds. The baby's simple pronunciation is merely his line of least resistance, the direct result of weight being tossed about by abundant vitality — *relaxation* coupled with *power.* "A bouncing baby!" we say.

Now, if we will only *let* it, the same law will work through the adult body. Our problem is to go back to the beginning and find again that *law,* then let it guide us. Having consciously set up the conditions of *feeling and hearing* of a healthy infant, we experience in speaking and in singing the sensation of a *moving stream of breath* — an inaudible "H" — upon which all sounds, consonants as well as vowels, travel. With this simple discovery, the student has put his finger upon the precious quality of *motion.* Herein lies that element generally recognized as "charm." A singer who possesses it is said to have "a floating voice," "an interesting voice," "a moving voice." And only that singer or actor who has found this simple magic talisman[1] can "live the song" or "live the part" and convey a genuine message to his audience.

Once again, we find ourselves examining first principles — the setting up of right conditions of *feeling and hearing* as stated first in Chapter Two. *Power working through relaxation coupled with the hearing of pure vowels* emerges then as the actual foundation of *motion* in the voice, or, as the old Italian masters called it, *singing*

---

[1] Ethel Barrymore found it early in life and so did her brothers Lionel and John.

on the breath. Once established, these right conditions become the basis of all natural, noble speech or song.

The *moving breath stream* is the active vehicle that carries quite impersonally anything the speaker or singer chooses to confide to its care, irrespective of language or accent. It is like an escalator, always moving, and only valuable when in motion. An escalator is impersonal; it waits for nobody, plays no favorites, carries not only people of all races, colors, creeds, but also all their *bundles.* It serves all with equal efficiency, can be neither hurried nor held back, and shoves both people and bundles off at the top without concern. The people riding on the escalator at the same time share for the moment the same fate. No matter what their personal desires, they are all subject to the *Law of the Escalator.* If they submit with a good grace, the law will serve them well, but if they attempt to flaunt the law, it can harm them quite ruthlessly.[2]

Now, our vocal escalator — our perpetually moving *breath stream* — carries upon it all day long, whenever we speak or sing, vowels, vowels, vowels as passengers. They vary greatly in many ways: in pronunciation, in size, in color, in dynamic force, in emotion, etc. But no matter how different these vowels, they share the same fate and are subject to the same *law* while they are grouped together upon our escalator — while we are speaking or singing a given phrase.

Most of the vowels carry *bundles.* These packages are the consonants, and no matter how many of them a passenger may possess, the escalator is equally kind or cruel to all. It will land passengers and their bundles safely at the top if it is allowed to carry them in its own comfortable way — unhurried, unslackened, while they (both vowels and consonants) rest at ease, abiding by the *Law of the Escalator.*

---

[2] I once heard of a tiny child who wanted to "find out where it went" and so inserted its wee fingers into the small crack covering the disappearing floor. What followed need not be described.

Until they learn better ways, these different passengers may be too interested in one another's packages. This is against the Law of the Escalator which decrees that, for all languages, the *vowels must* carry their *consonant bundles* in their *left arms,* leaving their right arms free.[3] The law forbids any passenger to use his right arm for any purpose whatsoever.[4] This prevents his possible interference with his neighbor's bundles, and also prevents his being interested in the final bundle of consonants (belonging to no vowel) which often closes a phrase, and which the *escalator,* with the assistance of its servant (the loosely hanging *jaw*) unconcernedly dumps at the top.[5] Passengers who insist upon using their right arms cause a great deal of confusion and strife. Such behavior may even stop the escalator temporarily.[6]

If the student has maintained the primary conditions of *feeling and hearing,* he will notice that a very essential part of the escalator machinery — the lower jaw — seems to hang heavily even when it is moving rapidly. Because of this, he will observe that each vowel, along with its consonant bundle or bundles, is accompanied by an *instantaneous* rising and falling of the weighty jaw. This action is merely a practical example of the detailed description, given in Chapter Nine, of the behavior of the head mechanism when vowels coupled with consonants are spoken in a steady stream.

The escalator analogy may be carried yet further. Even as an invisible but powerful motor runs the usual escalator, so our active, vitalized *breath stream escalator* is served by a physical motor which represents the harmonious cooperation of the *entire body.* This activity is discussed in detail in Chapter Ten.

---

[3] See Chapter 4, page 27.

[4] This results in a perfect *legato* in speech and song.

[5] The blocked out quotations at the close of Chapter 4 (The Foundation of Good English Diction) will serve as illustrations.

[6] See Chapter 10 concerning the *grunt.*

CHAPTER NINE

RESONANCE AND SOUND

How the Machine Works *Above* the Collar Bones

It is evident that our next concern must be the practical application of the ideas set forth in the foregoing chapters. For the
moment, let us devote our attention exclusively to *listening*.

As you sit in a straight chair, allow your entire body to slump
very heavily, being certain that it slumps *open* against the back of
the chair instead of converging towards an imaginary front prop.

Speak the Italian vowel "A" in the simplest, most childlike manner possible. An adult would tend to darken the vowel toward A3.[1]
But you are to pronounce a flat, white "A", approaching A2, which
sounds like a baby saying "ma-ma." Do not let it be "round" or
"pretty." Let it come out like a sigh — as though you were finishing
a yawn — "Ah." The American Middle Westerners use this bright
A in the word "hot," prolonging the vowel into a slight drone. Harvard students use it in the first syllable of their college yell, the consonant "r" being actually unspoken: "Harvard, Harvard, Harvard."

Now put the consonant f before A, and drone this syllable re-
peatedly in one connected stream — fA-fA-fA, being sure not to let
the repeated syllable break the streaming tone line. Before uttering
a sound, be certain that jaw and tongue are hanging heavily *and do
not change this condition.* Now *hear* this childishly, *breathily* spoken

---

[1] See Chapter 4, page 23.

61

syllable "fA-fA-fA-fA" *being uttered* through this formless machine, uttered as lazily as possible, and hence with lightning-fast action. This sounds paradoxical until you realize that the heavy jaw will hang until you hear the syllable. The articulation of the consonant f, ordered by the ear, has lifted the heavy, unwilling jaw in spite of itself, and, because there is no reason for its staying up, it flops open again heavily the instant you hear "A."

This necessarily cumbersome description must not lead you to think that f and A are pronounced separately. On the contrary, you must hear them spoken simultaneously, as though they were inextricable.

Now, suppose you add two syllables to fA and make it fA-nA-lA. Before beginning to talk these three syllables, let your heavy jaw hang quite foolishly. Out of this shapelessness comes fA, hanging into the easy, natural smile (the upper teeth showing readily) that is necessary to this almost white vowel pronunciation. While keeping your jaw heavy in order to preserve this A form, allow nA to hoist it for the briefest possible fraction of time (just long enough to articulate a very careless n). Then let it fall again of its own sheer weight into the A form. This entire closing-and-opening process is accomplished in the twinkling of an eye. The same process takes care of the third syllable, lA.

You will notice that the tongue is involved in the second and third syllables (nA and lA) only. Be sure that it *feels* thick and lazy, as though it were unwilling to make the slightest effort to articulate n and l without the jaw. On the contrary, it is not at all averse to "getting a ride" up and down on the rapidly moving though lazy jaw, and by this means both consonants "get spoken" without the tongue losing contact with the lower lip.

You will observe that the tip of the tongue does not participate in this articulation at all, but that the portion just behind the tip touches the inner side of the upper teeth when you speak these consonants.

Now speak this group of syllables (fA-nA-lA) four times in one connected stream. Speak them childishly and somewhat breathily, as though more breath than voice were spilling out of your mouth: "fA-nA-lA fA-nA-lA fA-nA-lA fA-nA-lA." Let the pitch move indefinitely up and down, not dwelling in any one spot. If you have a metronome, set it at about 132 and speak one syllable for each stroke.

From the very beginning of your study you should be tireless in your determination to *rest in each vowel form* until the *hearing* of the next syllable *compels* that form to change. Finally you come to the last sound to be uttered—lA of the final group. Keep such a heavy jaw that the A position is assured even *after* the sound has ceased. When this occurs, you will find yourself immediately and instinctively "breathing into the last form or position," as I term it. This simple but invaluable habit is well worth cultivating from the very start for, if firmly established, it precludes any such thing as a "breath problem."[2]

Let us now apply the same ideas to the next vowel, E.[3] We hear it in the word "met" and in the first syllable of "Edward." Do not pronounce it "Ei" as in "hay." Listen attentively while you say "fE-nE-lE" four times, roaming about in pitch and speaking childishly and breathily in one joined stream of sound as you did with fA-nA-lA. Allow the form of the last lE to remain unchanged until you have "breathed into it." When spoken properly the vowel E may seem very shrill to you. It will match in quality the pronunciation of the ultra bright A, which was almost A2. You will find the heavy lips do not need to smile. In fact, their inclination seems to be to hang in a rather stupid pout.

Consider the vowel I (pronounced as in "machine") from the same standpoint and put an f before it. It should not be pronounced like

---

[2] See Chapter 10, p. 73.

[3] Remember that we are going to use the Italian pronunciation, "eh." See Table, p. 21.

the vowel in "fish" or "finish." Instead, hear yourself pronouncing it "fee." It is the shrillest sounding vowel of all, and it is not easy, as a rule, for Americans to *permit* this piercing, sharp vowel to come through unaltered. Subconsciously we seem to want to soften it, to "make it prettier." Bear in mind that our *only* concern, aurally speaking, is to listen for the *purest possible vowel pronunciation,* and if this brings with it an unaccustomed shrillness and edginess of tone quality, *we* at least are not responsible. We have done our best in pronouncing truly. What is happening is at least perfectly comfortable and effortless, so we may as well get used to it. Actually, to other people our new "queer sound" will seem quite what it should be, a free, pure, *natural* vowel. Possibly, for a little while, you will have to be on guard to keep the same condition of heaviness in jaw, mouth, and tongue while speaking I. But, as you experiment, you will discover that it, too, seems to require a feeling of heavy, pouting, unsmiling lips, less open than for E, but with the tongue remaining, as always, heavy and a unit with the lower lip. Speak "fI-nI-lI" four times through the moderate range of the conversation voice, not forgetting to *breathe into the last form,* "lI."

In setting up the same basic conditions for O, be very careful not to say "O-u." Nor should you permit "A3." An Irishman, speaking the words "Only" and "sO," would give the exact pronunciation. The Scandinavians, too, have the same pure sound in "Å." Do not make your lips into a round hole. Follow the line of least resistance and "let the sound come through formlessness." Then you will discover that a sort of "straight line mouth," showing the teeth slightly in a loose smile (like the position for "A," closed into a line), is what nature wants to create for the clear speaking of this particular vowel. If you were an Italian, you would take the mouth form more or less for granted. As the result of your having right conditions of hearing, the pure sound would be accompanied spontaneously and of necessity with the correct form. *As a matter of fact, this is the habit you have started out to cultivate.*

Perhaps it will help to approach this problem of the pronunciation of O from a different angle. Try speaking it before a mirror exactly as we do in English, being careful to avoid the diphthong-ending "u." Prolong the sound, O, and do not end it with the corners of the lips either falling or approaching each other. Instead, keep the *exact form* (not a round hole, but a loosely smiling straight mouth) that accompanies the initiation of this vowel sound. (I am going into such detail about this vowel because pure O occurs in our language only as dialect.[4]) Speak "fO-nO-lO" according to the same principle employed in speaking the preceding syllables. Do not fail to breathe into the last form, "lO."

If you can imitate the loose "MOO" of a cow, or the blowing of the wind, "OO," you will arrive at the correct pronunciation of the Italian "U," which has needlessly become a difficult sound for many in our country. It may be helpful if I tell you what *not* to hear. It is hard to describe the distorted sound most Americans produce when they try to pronounce this vowel. They start with an impure I, pass for the briefest instant through a sound resembling the vowel Ö,[5] then wind up in an imperfect Ü.[6] As you speak it in a prolonged stream, moving about in pitch, be certain that you are hearing only *one* pure, unchanging vowel. The result may sound amazingly weak, but *never* try to make it otherwise. Keep on faithfully attending to your real business—the patient, persistent setting up of right conditions. The lips naturally assume a loose, unpuckered whistling shape, somewhat pouty, and of course the thick and weighty tongue remains undisturbed in its oneness with the lower lip. Say "fU-nU-lU" four times, being careful to "rest in the vowel form" and to let the rapidly moving, heavily hanging jaw do *all* the work in articulating consonants while the undisturbed tongue lies dormant. In speaking these U syllables, the vowel forms remain hanging *always,* just as they did

---

4 See Chapter 4, page 25.
5 See Chapter 5, page 35.
6 See Chapter 5, page 35.

for the more open sounds. Be very sure that you experience this simple truth and remember to let the breath go by itself into the last lU form.

It should be evident that what applies to one vowel applies to all. If you have found that your heavy head and face *form themselves to best advantage* in accordance with the sound your ear is demanding, then you will be convinced that *you have no power successfully to arrange the forms* through which these vowels come. Nature neither wants nor needs your help, and if you insist upon lending your aid, trouble begins. Acquire the habit of establishing the same conditions of *feeling and hearing* throughout the entire vocal range no matter what vowel is uttered.

The foregoing exercises suggest an indefinite number of others. One that naturally follows would be: fA-nA-lA fE-nE-lE fA-nA-lA fE-nE-lE, etc. Groups with three vowels would come next, then groups with four, and finally: fA-nA-lA fE-nE-lE fI-nI-lI fO-nO-lO fU-nU-lU fA-nA-lA. In every case, be certain to "breathe into the last form," whatever it may be. Set the metronome at about 60 and allow one beat for each group of three sounds.

Appended is a table of single consonants and consonant clusters for creating further syllables for practice. They are placed in orderly groups for convenient reference. Remember that the conditions of feeling *never change,* no matter what vowel or consonant sound you listen for, or what form Nature is creating that that sound may come through.

TABLE OF CONSONANTS AND CONSONANT CLUSTERS

Sounds involving upper lip and under lip:
M B P

Sounds involving upper front teeth and lower lip:
F V

Sounds involving edges of upper front teeth and tongue:

TH & TH
1 2

Sounds involving inner sides of front upper teeth, foremost portion of hard palate and tongue, just behind the tip:

D T L N

Sounds involving foremost portion of hard palate and tongue tip:

R (rolled)

Sounds involving soft palate and thick of tongue:

NG K G

Sounds causing tongue to lose contact with the lower lip:

S Z CH SH ZH J R

Common consonant clusters:

**BL FL GL KL ML PL SL VL SHL THL
BR DR FR GR KR MR PR TR VR
THR STR ST SHT**

Old Italian syllables (useful in creating speaking and singing exercises):

BE DA ME NI PO TU LA

CHAPTER TEN

RESONANCE AND BREATH

How the Machine Works *Below* the Collar Bones

In Chapters One and Three I referred to right breathing as one of the *results* that follow the *establishment of proper singing conditions*. How are singers to find the right way to breathe—the baby's way, the natural way? The most direct approach to this subtle and little-understood subject is to determine what conditions should *not* be set up for natural breathing. This should lead us to positive conclusions.

One consequence of wrong breathing I call the *grunt*. Unfortunately this affliction is shared by so many of our opera, concert, and radio stars that the world accepts it without comment. It ends nearly every phrase these people sing, its intensity being in direct proportion to the intensity of that phrase. It hardly seems possible that the *grunt* could be considered a thing of beauty or an aid to interpretation. True, the *grunt* is a useful and fitting bit of stage business, and claims a legitimate place when, for instance, Canio sobs out his grief, or when a heroine is being strangled and manages to sing throughout the ordeal. But when the *grunt* stops being a sparingly used tool and becomes an almost universal habit, it is time critics gave it serious consideration.

What *causes* the *grunt?* Its immediate occasion is a spasmodic collapse of the throat resulting in a violent disturbance of the vocal cords. These snap together suddenly, then instantly separate, allowing a gushing escape of breath before the next inhalation. This momentary spasm of the mechanism *above* the collar bones is directly and intimately connected with what goes on below them.

How would the throat behave if there were no grunt at the end of a phrase? There would be no change in the shape of the singer's throat and no closing of jaws at the moment of inhalation. Instead, he would find himself *breathing into the plastic mouth form[1]* of the final vowel of the phrase, regardless of whether or not that vowel is followed by a consonant or consonant cluster.[2] *The music of the phrase* would be the only audible sound,[3] and the singer would find himself ready for the next phrase without further preparation. In short, he would have set up and then maintained *right conditions* throughout his singing of every phrase and the subsequent intake of the breath. The process of breathing would have gone on as naturally and correctly as it does with babies.

The body seeks consistency throughout, whether for good or ill. Wrong conditions hang together as consistently as right ones. Discomfort and strain *above* the collar bones have their counterpart

---

[1] Whenever possible the breath should be taken through the nose, or through nose and mouth together. This act does not, however, affect the position of the mouth and hanging jaw.

[2] See Chapter 9, page 63, end of the vowel A.

[3] The singer who grunts at the end of phrases often commences with a *lurch,* which, being a throat attack, is akin to the *grunt.* In time this unfortunate habit creeps into and persists throughout all his phrases, and we hear a "throat attack" on syllables in the middle of phrases, commencing with a vowel or with a singable consonant. Although he may be young in years, his voice sounds "old," the charm is gone. There are and have been a few great singers whose voices have remained "young" long past middle life. Maggie Teyte, Dan Beddoe, Plunkett Greene, Battistini, De Luca, Calvé, Lilli Lehmann, Ida Auer-Herbeck, Patti, Chaliapin — these are some who in their old age have delighted me with their youthful singing.

below. The grunter has been taught to "sing from the diaphragm," and fancies that by stiffening his abdomen he is achieving something called "support." He is woefully mistaken. With the stiffened abdomen come stiff knees, hips, shoulders, sides, jaws, face, and throat—in short, a static condition[4] of the whole body.

The entire body must work in a state of harmonious activity. This is possible only when we have *completely relaxed* and have achieved a feeling of utter heaviness. Muscles and joints feel like open hands. *Relaxation,*[5] not clenched fists, is the basic condition, and this feeling must be maintained continuously. When the student has sensed this relaxation, this heaviness, he is ready to discover the vitality that can lift it. To the good singer, these two are the Siamese twins. A practical example of this double principle of *power working through relaxation* will be found in Chapter One, pages 8-9 and again in Chapter Three, page 17.

Turning back to the "chair exercise," let us study the action of *power*—life, vitality, energy—as it lifts the weighty, relaxed body up out of the chair. The desire to arise *without throwing the weight*

---

[4] When I hear singers who cannot perform without a pained face or a fixed grin or knit brows, or who must go through lip and jaw contortions in order to make the text understood, or who have no control over the stiff gyrations of their hands, I know that, to a greater or lesser degree, there is a static condition of their entire bodies, including the head and neck mechanism. As a result, the sound of their voices is also static (*non legato*), hard, uninteresting, without flow or motion. They are unable to alter this state of affairs unless they are *willing* consciously to set up the conditions a baby does spontaneously. This step requires a great degree of courage and humility, but if singers are big enough and wise enough to take it, they will presently find that all things are possible. One inevitable result of consistent stiffness is a *tremolo* — a tight quiver.

[5] It must be clearly understood, however, that relaxation is never an end in itself, but rather a means to an end. While *power* can manifest itself *only* through relaxation, *relaxation* can manifest itself without *power*. The very same relaxation characterizes a drunken man, an idiot, and a baby, and it is a common saying that these do not hurt themselves when they fall. But the drunken man and the idiot are relaxed and *impotent*, while the baby is relaxed and at the same time is charged with abundant life, vitality, *power*.

forward prompts a spontaneous and strong pressure (a push or dig) into the floor. The immediate reaction to this push is the sensation of strong and vital *pull*. It is as though an elastic line, starting at the floor, stretches to the top of the head.. The body assembles itself, coordinates, about this line, and a rotating chain of *motion* begins. The *line, pull,* brings into being the coordination that results in *power,* which in turn guarantees the maintenance of that *line.*

Let us study this vitality in greater detail. What does it do to our bodies? What do we *feel* in getting up from the chair as I have described? What are our sensations?

With our feeling of a mighty *pull* up from the pushing feet, the thigh and buttock muscles tuck down and under into the chair seat. If we do not yield to temptation and throw the weight forward, we feel these big muscles pulling towards each other in a tremendous effort to *lift* the heavy torso. After a struggle we find ourselves standing and experiencing a wonderful sensation of equilibrium, levitation, balance—what I call *power* working through *relaxation*. This happy state[6] is the result of our having set up right conditions, and it will remain with us as long as we maintain them continuously. This approach underlies the correct, free functioning of man's innumerable physical activities, of which singing is merely one.

The thigh and buttock muscles are the heaviest in the body. They support and govern everything above and below them, the legs, torso, neck, and head. This feeling of support is shared by the shoulders. which, turning in their relaxed, open joints, draw together and down to a center back. The sides, along the ribs (so inactive and dead in most of us), also turn, and play a very important part in this life-activity. The knees and everything below them, being "the support below the support," are just as active.

---

[6] Many a beginning student has remarked, on successfully accomplishing this difficult and most important exercise: "What a wonderful feeling! I have never felt like this before. I feel balanced on top of the world, ready to do anything!"

It appears then, that this sensation of the *entire length* of the sides turning downward towards a common center at the back results in the feeling there of a column, prop, center, support, to which the body is continually relaxing and turning.[7] This impels the *push* of the feet, which in turn creates the *"pull* from below." This action further requires that in the body there shall be a drawing away of everything from a center front to a center back, and so on. This rotating *cha:n of activity,* already described on page 71, is continuous during singing, whether one is exhaling or inhaling. It never for a moment becomes static.[8]

Having established the conditions for right breathing, what is there to say about inhaling and exhaling, about the act of breathing itself? Actually, very little indeed. But that little is exceedingly important. Being alive, you breathe, and because you are consciously maintaining the conditions of a healthy infant, your results are the same and your breath is naturally deep. Singers and singing teachers agree that babies have the secret of "deep breathing"; yet this is an open secret, free to all who will really try to find it.

As a young woman I was much disturbed by the term "deep breathing." What did it really mean? Everyone who used this expression sounded learned and profound, but no one could give me a clear answer. I thought to myself: "Well, some day, when I get to Europe, I shall surely find out what this 'deep breathing' is." Fortunately when I arrived there I discovered Ida Auer-Herbeck, who taught me *how to think.* That is really all a good teacher can do for a pupil. I realized gradually that there was no such thing as "deep breathing" per se. In singing, we have no direct control over the organs involved in breathing, and there is no magic way of inhaling and exhaling, no secret recipe, no bag of tricks to help us out. Instead I found a better

---

[7] A well coordinated young man — a beginner with a great vocal gift — once declared, "If only I can remember to lean back on that strong *prop,* then there's nothing *to* the singing, it's so easy."

[8] Being an instinctive life-activity, all this is quite beyond the conscious control

and more accurate expression—"deep *preparation* for the breath."
"Deep breathing," then, is a *result*. The cause governing this result
is *power* working through *relaxation* and we are the ones who can
and *must* set up these conditions.[9]

There are two things that should become habits. The first I call
"rhythmic breathing." We should never try to hold a deep breath.
Babies do nothing unnatural; neither should we. Instead, when we
are about to sing, the breath should be moving in and out. There
should never be a static moment in this life activity; we should
never "hold the breath," never "breathe, hold, sing." Such a sequence
precludes rhythmic breathing. Instead, we should make use of
what I term "breath timing." Breath timing is the precise aware-
ness of *when* to inhale before beginning a phrase, whether that
phrase opens a song or follows an interlude of accompaniment. During
such an interlude, after "breathing into the form of the last vowel
sound"[10] of the foregoing phrase, the singer should not become static
for the rest of the pause and then "snatch a breath" just as he is about
to sing again. On the contrary, the breath that is taken "into the
form" is succeeded by an exhalation and this by an inhalation, and
so on, without one static moment occurring between any of them.
The student must find out for himself precisely how many unhurried
inhalations and exhalations will naturally fill a given interlude, so
that the final leisurely inhalation will be instantaneously followed by
the attack on the next phrase.

Bad results often come from wrong preparation for a phrase.

---

of man. One thing is certain though: nature cannot work through us until we set
up right conditions. Whether we are consciously doing so or not, we are *always*
setting up conditions of some sort, and here our control — our responsibility —
begins and ends. The only way we can reach the inside body and its behavior is
through the outside body.

[9] "All voice teachers have the same goal — beautiful singing; and all of us recognize
it when we hear it. The difference between other teachers and myself is that they
work with results, while I am working with causes." — I.A.-H.

[10] See Chapter 9, page 63, last sentence under the vowel "A."

"Breathe, hold, sing" or "Static, grab-a-breath, sing"—both ruin good singing.[11] All one needs to insure noble, natural singing are the simple words "Breathe and sing." They apply to any style of singing, from Mozart to Wagner, from the classics to ultra modern compositions. Succeeding phrases in a song present no difficulties.[12]

---

[11] Perhaps the reader has already surmised that this habit is closely connected with the *lurch* and *grunt,* two of its most flagrant results.

[12] An excellent study for training beginners to "breathe into the form, then attack from that form" may be found in Vaccai, *Practical Method* (Schirmer's Library of Musical Classics), page 10, Lesson 5.

CHAPTER ELEVEN

THE MOUTH POSITIONS

Chapter Nine dealt with the behavior of the head mechanism when vowels and consonants are articulated through the usual octave-wide range of the speaking voice. But what about singing or calling, when the voice exceeds these more or less definite boundaries? What, if anything, happens?

An experiment in physics may give us a clue. Hold a vibrating tuning fork at the mouth of an empty jar. The tone is slightly reinforced by the size of the air space within. Now pour water slowly into the jar. Notice that the tone increases in volume until it reaches its maximum. If you continue to pour in water, the tone will gradually grow fainter again. This demonstrates that for every pitch there exists an air chamber exactly suited in size to its maximum enhancement.

Whenever we speak, we make unconscious use of the same principle. Let us say, for example, that you are talking to a person near you whose name is Ida or Alice or Arthur. As you speak the "A," the stressed vowel sound in these names, your mouth opens slightly more than when you pronounce the other fundamental vowels (E, I, O and U). But if one of these people is a short distance away and you wish to attract his attention, without a thought you raise the pitch of your voice considerably so that the sound vibrations will carry to the ear of your friend. When you call, your jaw will drop as you utter the first syllable, and your mouth will stretch somewhat into an easy smile, probably showing most of your teeth. Why should

75

this be so? Because instinctively you seek a larger air chamber, one better suited to reinforce the raised pitch. So natural, so unconscious is this process that you never give it a thought.

Singing is merely a conscious refining of this instinctive shouting.[1] It may be said that singing is finding the best mouth position for any vowel sound on any pitch.

Although individual singing voices differ widely, all voices can be grouped roughly as high, middle, and low. Such classification of a given voice is often merely a personal opinion. I can think of several singers whose naturally wide and even ranges made them difficult to classify. Calvé, Jean de Reszke, Louis Graveure, Sigrid Onegin, and Karl Planck are examples that come to my mind. In my own teaching experience I have sometimes classified as "high" a voice that later grew freer and hence more resonant, and re-classified itself as "middle" (and vice versa).

A man's bass, baritone, or tenor voice corresponds to a woman's contralto, mezzo, or soprano. All are trained the same way because all are human instruments. When a boy's voice "changes" it drops one octave in pitch. At maturity girls' voices "change" also, but they do not alter in pitch.

It is important to note what happens to our voice machine when we send absolutely pure vowels up or down the entire range. Not forgetting the right habits of listening and feeling,[2] let us consider first the pure vowel A.

In fairly high voices (sopranos and tenors) the heart of the speaking voice extends from E♭ (first line, G-clef) up through A (second space).[3] That of mezzos and baritones extends from D (first

---

[1] J. C. Cooper was fond of posing the following question to a new pupil: "What's singin'? Give me a definition of singin'!" "Well," a student once thoughtfully ventured, "perhaps it might be called 'speaking in tune'." Whatever the answer, it was certain to be met with a violent shaking of the head and "No, no! I can give you a definition of singin' in just two words. Singin's refined hollerin', that's what it is — refined hollerin'!"

[2] See Chapter 3.

[3] Male voices one octave lower in all cases.

space below the staff, G-clef) through A♭ (second space), and contraltos and basses seem to range from C♯ (first added line below the staff, G-clef) through F♯ (first space in the staff). Since we are dealing with the human instrument — a slightly varying factor — it should be remembered that these measurements, while fairly accurate, are never fixed.

In this speaking portion of the range, the vowel A causes the mouth to open only slightly, as it does in conversation. If it is pronounced correctly the mouth will smile somewhat,[4] regardless of the type of voice. Beginning usually at B♭, third line G-clef (middle voices at A, low voices at G) and ascending chromatically, high voices open the mouth more and more with each half-step, the loose, relaxed jaw dropping almost imperceptibly. Each "drop" is barely distinguishable to the eye, but the singer is thoroughly aware of these fractional distances. At the beginning, the smiling mouth is relatively small and the vocal range relatively large. When the singer ascends to B♭ (second space above the staff), however, the difference between the necessarily wide open, laughing mouth and the slightly open smiling mouth needed an octave lower is marked. All the world acknowledges: "Of course the mouth opens wider as one sings higher."

Actually, the correct mouth position is *felt* more accurately by the singer than it can be *seen* by the teacher. The teacher, guided more surely by what he *hears* than by what he *sees,* may tell the pupil "not to open so much" when singing the vowel A on a given pitch, or else "open a trifle more." Such advice is indispensable for the beginning student who knows little or nothing about what he is to hear and feel. When a singer is sufficiently advanced to hear and feel that a tone is *right,* the mouth position he spontaneously takes in singing that tone is bound to be correct.

It must not be forgotten therefore that the highest authority respecting the vocal instrument of any given pupil is the *feeling and*

---

[4] See Chapter 9.

hearing of the pupil himself. The wise and watchful teacher can distinguish between a genuine vocal discovery on the part of the student, and mere waywardness masquerading (unconsciously, of course) as independence and original thought. The teacher will never dictate to such a student, and will have endless patience while he watches him investigate numerous "blind alleys." Who knows but that one such independent excursion may one day unearth a real treasure, to the enrichment of all concerned!

The pure vowel A has one peculiarity not shared by the other vowels. When going *down* the range chromatically, *below* the speaking-voice area, A seems to open the mouth more and more. High voices start opening at D, first space below the staff, G-clef (middle voices at C♯, low voices at C). As the voice proceeds downward by semitones, the smiling mouth instinctively opens wider and wider. In this lower, shorter portion of the vocal range, the mouth opens less subtly. Low A (second leger line below the staff) has approximately the same mouth position as high A (first leger line above the staff).

The mouth positions for the remaining pure vowels are less complicated than those for the vowel A. In the lowest portion of the range none of them opens the mouth any wider than when singing in the speaking region.

E (see Chapter Nine) comes through a heavy, pouting mouth until a certain pitch is reached. Then, in order to preserve the identity of the vowel (coming through an unchanging throat), the mouth position begins to alter. High voices usually feel the need for this change on C (third space), middle voices about on B or B♭, lowest voices about on A. From an almost imperceptible dropping open of the jaw at the first altered position, the voice rises by semitones while the mouth hangs, little by little, into an easy casual smile. When high voices reach G above the staff (singing the vowel E) the *external* mouth position is practically the same as that for the vowel A, middle and low voices in proportion. *Inside* the mouth there is a marked difference. The absolutely relaxed tongue (always lying over the lower front teeth for *all vowels* and *all pitches*) which lay like a rug throughout the entire range while A was sung, is thick and soft when E is sung, and grows thicker and higher as the range is ascended. If the singer is singing through a relaxed, unchanging throat, the pronunciation of the vowel E will remain unchanged. His flabby, soft tongue feels as though it were almost too big for his mouth by the time he reaches his top tones.

We find that the vowel I (see Chapter Nine) has much in common with the vowel E. It too comes through a thick, pouty mouth, *less* open than when E is sung. As our voices rise, we reach a pitch where either the mouth or the throat and vowel must change. The *integrity of the vowel pronunciation* must be maintained; and so we find our lips *beginning* to smile when this pitch is reached—D fourth line with high voices, C third space with middle voices, B♭ with lowest voices. This scarcely detectable smile increases slightly with each semitone until finally, at the top of the range, the singer feels as though his entire face, including his nose, is smiling. If not interfered with, the tongue will ride very high, even higher than when singing E. And if the vowel pronunciation is pure, the tone will sound extremely shrill to the singer, although quite right to outside ears. The resemblance in form between E and I ends where the mouth positions begin to change; whereas E *both* hangs and smiles, I merely smiles.

O is closely related to A from the standpoint both of mouth positions and of pronunciation (see Chapter Nine). Perhaps it is a help to think of O as a "closed up A," closed loosely into a straight line. But in ascending the range, we arrive at a pitch where O too begins to alter the shape of the mouth. Oddly enough, this point will be the very same pitch where E began to change the mouth from a somewhat closed and "cross" position to one that was hanging and more pleasant in feeling. In singing O throughout the upper range, the singer must be very sure to hang into a new, *fresh* smile with each succeeding semitone. If he thinks *only* of dropping his jaw and not of smiling at the same time, then the opening mouth will *lose* the faint smile maintained throughout the middle range, the throat will change its shape, and the pure vowel will be lost. Externally, in the top part of the range, the *appearance* of the singer's mouth when singing A, E, and O is practically the same.

In a way, U is the simplest vowel of all to sing. It maintains the *same* lip position throughout the range, although the loose jaw drops to some extent when ascending above the speaking voice region (see Chapter Nine). The pronunciation of this vowel is *entirely* dependent upon the form the lips take. The form taken by the lips will be right if the pure vowel U is maintained and the entire mechanism, including the lips, remains plastic.

The same is of course true respecting every vowel sound. When a singer *feels* aright and, simultaneously, *hears* the correct pronunciation of a given vowel, both the tone he is singing at the moment and the mouth position it calls for are bound to be correct. If he is plastic and relaxed and at the same time is full of vitality and power, the singer always *feels* as though the tone opens or closes the mouth *for him*. He merely gives the order.

CHAPTER TWELVE

CONCLUSION

Those ancient empiricists, the old Italian singing masters, left to posterity only a few scattered hints concerning their opinions on this much mooted subject. It seems odd that such phrases as "support the voice" and "sing on the breath" should ever be misunderstood or misconstrued by teachers with a resulting discomfort to their pupils. However, if we can discover the *point of view* of those great teachers of the "golden age of song," we shall find that they were merely emphasizing an instinctive process that was then and remains today an open secret.

Natural singing disappeared from the world with Manuel García's invention of the laryngoscope. García (the most famous voice teacher of the last century) was beset with an anatomist's desire to "see the wheels go round." He wanted to observe the action of his pupils' vocal cords. His invention, though a curse to singers, has been a most useful tool to dentists and throat specialists.

The advent of the "Scientific Age" had a detrimental and lasting effect upon singers. Singing teachers and their pupils, looking for a scientific short-cut to their goal, determined to *make* results to their liking instead of *supplying causes for results* to follow. Singers have become more and more involved in the consequent confusion, until today a truly "great singer" who reaches the heights and depths of emotional expression is a rarity.

To the human voice, the most personal of musical instruments, the poet entrusts his words and the composer his music. Artistic singing must be measured by the singer's success in fulfilling this double duty. But to many a singer, even to some who have enjoyed great worldly success, a song or an aria is merely an opportunity for showing off his particular instrument. The artist who places himself wholly and unreservedly at the disposal of both poet and composer is rare. Such a singer actually re-creates a song, and is one of the great people of all time.

These days singers are too often "made great" by well organized advertising and "ballyhoo." All of these people began with better than average voices. How strange and how tragic that schooling should have dulled rather than enhanced the natural beauty of their voices!

Good schooling manifests itself in a perfect balance of breath and resonance. This in turn results in good intonation, perfect control of dynamics, a range of two and a half to three octaves or more, perfect diction, evenness of voice, beauty of quality, so-called "breath control"—in a word, *natural singing*. Every voice can then develop to its utmost and become a worthy instrument for human expression. Some fairly ordinary voices can develop extraordinary qualities. They are like violins played by a master. I would rather hear a master play on a cheap fiddle than a fool on a Stradivarius.

Motion—the balance of resonance and breath—carries every tone sung by a great singer. If the listener is exacting, his ear will be gratified by a fidelity to pitch as constant as that expected of a violinist. He will never hear a forced or driven tone, or a throaty attack at the opening of phrases. No "grunts," great or small, offend him at the end of phrases, and there will be no gasping noise when the singer inhales.

The listener relaxes in his chair, losing himself in what the words and music have to convey, because the singer is physically and mentally equal to his task.

ADDENDUM

Following is a translation from the original German of a letter written to me by Ida Auer-Herbeck during my student days:

Dresden
September 24, 1906

It is a good sign that the middle register is now becoming deeper supported. From this deep basis, seek unification at the center (prop support) of all the strength of the sides. This is possible because you are allowing the side joints to relax towards the *entire back column* from the feet up (pillar, center, prop, support). Now, while maintaining the connection between the foundation of this back prop and the nose, you are able to exhale without any cessation of this life-activity and without any part becoming stiff or weak. Then it must happen that this "pull" [up] to the depths of the chest (the center), under the breast bone, is achieved, nevermore to depart. More and more a "pull" from below, out of the firmly standing heels! I have explained it so often and in various ways, have I not? And it can *seem* ever so clear, and yet so often be unsuccessful in the doing. But it is certain that in this way the body assembles itself together [coordinates] for the expression of the soul, thereby revealing the singing instrument (and the management thereof) that leads to great natural voice expression.

PART II

HOW TO USE THE TOOLS
FOR
SPEAKING AND SINGING

LESSON I

The old Italian *maestri* were undoubtedly sound in their counsel: "Sing as you speak."[1] But to this advice must now be added the qualification: "IF you speak correctly."

Before we combine voice with music, let us isolate the five pure Italian vowels and speak them in combination with consonants and consonant clusters.[2] This is accomplished with ease when right conditions of feeling and listening have been set up. This first step has been explained in minute detail in Chapter Nine. Your first voice lesson will consist of a thorough review of that chapter. It will take many hours of conscientious practice before the *principle* therein exemplified becomes your own. But when you have accomplished this, you will have gone a long way towards mastering obvious problems when you begin to use the singing voice. The tools for correct

---

[1] The *speaking voice* and the *singing voice* are *one and the same*.
[2] See page 66.

diction, breathing, beginning and ending of phrases, and *legato* speaking and singing are all contained in that very first lesson.

When you have begun to make the *principle* involved in Chapter Nine your *speech habit,* it will be a comparatively easy matter, later, to transfer that same *principle* to the singing voice. Then you will realize, from your own experience, exactly what the old masters meant when they said, "Sing as you speak!"

It is so hard to be easy! You have set forth upon a path whose slogan might well be "Try not to try!" Being a potential artist, you may be inhibited by an artistic conscience that tends to stiffen you physically by its constant admonition to "be careful!" This painstaking trait can no more be changed than can the color of your eyes. It is possible, however, to put it to use. Why not be careful *to be careless?*

Do not minimize the fundamental importance of your first lesson, Chapter Nine. The exercises suggested there should be your daily diet for months to come, until they have actually become unconscious habit.

The "chair exercise" may be practiced to much advantage during the pre-singing days.[3] The sensation you experience in mastering this exercise actually comprises all there is to be said about setting up right conditions of *feeling* when singing. When performing it, be sure your jaw is not shut and stiff. Insist that it hang loosely open. If you repeat this exercise a hundred times each day, you will greatly strengthen the coordination of the entire body, thus helping build a singing instrument of *elastic power.*

---

[3] The "chair exercise" is described on pages 8-9, 17 and 70.

LESSON II

No matter how intelligent you may be, you will probably be more or less at sea concerning Chapter Nine when you come for your second lesson.

The mind receives ideas readily enough; it is another matter to induce the body to follow them through. The mind comprehends in a flash, and the body comes stumbling after. This is particularly true of the part of the body above the collar bones, the part with which we are first concerned. Never forget that the desired result can be obtained only if we set up *and then maintain* right conditions of feeling and hearing. *Feel* formless and heavy in tongue, mouth, and jaw, as though the tongue were too big for the mouth. *Listen* intently, keenly, for *pure vowels*.

Never grow weary of going over and over one single exercise until it begins to *flow of itself*. Patience and a practical sense of humor are indispensable factors, especially at first. Frequent lessons plus persistent practice are the only means of expediting the attainment of good speech habits. After that, singing is to a great degree easy. Almost daily lessons, at least for the first month, are an ideal arrangement. If this is not possible, then three lessons a week—never fewer than two.[1]

When Chapter Nine has been carefully taught and conscientiously practiced, you will have attained:

(1) The ability to begin every phrase with a relaxed, open jaw

---

[1] In the life of an ambitious, talented student the financial circumstances are often far from ideal. It is hoped that such difficulties may be mitigated to some extent by the *basic work* offered by this book. After a preliminary course of frequent lessons (as frequent as possible), the student should, with the help of this volume, be capable of *self instruction,* visiting the teacher once a week, or even less often.

(a fool's face) instead of beginning with a fixed consonant or vowel position.

(2) The ability to end every phrase by breathing into the mouth form[1] *created by the final vowel of the phrase,* instead of ending with a partially closed mouth and jaw, then breathing.

(3) The ability to rest both mouth and jaw quietly in each vowel form until the utterance of the next syllable changes their position, instead of anticipating the next consonant by going to *its* form ahead of time.

Hearing thus clearly emerges as the primary force that moves the jaw from one syllable to the next. The result of right hearing and right coordinating activity is therefore speech that is smooth, flowing, connected—as the Italians say, *"legato."*

Many years ago a student, D. (now noted for his impeccable diction), was going through the basic struggle of learning how to sing. It seemed almost impossible for him to grasp the idea of a relaxed jaw that was moved up and down, *by hearing,* for every single syllable.

I did my best to illustrate by speaking—first the wrong way (with immobile jaw), then the right way (the jaw tumbling from one syllable to the next). I did not hesitate to appear quite idiotic in my behavior, but apparently all to no purpose. "Some other time," I thought as, the lesson ended, I began on other tasks elsewhere.

Presently D. followed me, saying, "Now, Mrs. Beckman, I must go home." His voice sounded comically queer — like little marbles falling, one for every syllable. I was amazed to see my non-plastic pupil *permitting* his heavy jaw to flop up and down — exaggerated, uninhibited, and exactly as I had tried in vain to induce him to do a few minutes before!

---

[1] Though mouth position and tongue tip remain intact, the breath passes through the nose whenever possible. When inhalation must be accomplished rapidly, it passes through both nose and mouth together. If a phrase ends with a consonant or consonant cluster, the *mouth form* of the preceding vowel is instantaneously resumed, *after* the consonant or cluster has been uttered.

"D., that's exactly *right,* that *feeling!* Ridicule me, caricature me, mock me! Make a jest of these lessons! Not until you can be a buffoon can you be a singer!"

The clown in him had destroyed self-consciousness, rigidity; and I had not made a fool of myself in vain.

Perhaps a chart of D.'s words will make still clearer the behavior of his jaw. 1-2-3, 1-2-3, etc. represent the jaw's action when speaking or singing a phrase. Beginning at zero (a relaxed, open jaw — a fool's face), the heavy jaw is lifted to 1 by the pronunciation of the consonant n — *but only for a fraction of time.* Then the jaw drops heavily and instantaneously to 2 as the syllable nA (n and A spoken simultaneously) is heard. This same process repeats for each vowel (together with its consonant or cluster) until the final cluster (um) has been heard. Since there is no vowel connected with um, *the breath goes into the O form at 2,* and this completes the phrase.

The heavy horizontal lines (2 to 3) represent the duration of the vowel sounds, which are naturally longer or shorter, according to the requirements of the case.[2]

1	1	1	1	1	1	1	1	1	1
0 2—3ʹ	2—3ʹ	2—3ʹ	2—3ʹ	2—3ʹ	2—3ʹ	2—3ʹ	2—3ʹ	2—3ʹ	2
nA	umI	sE	zbE	kmA4	nA	imA4	stgO	uhO	um
now	mis	sez	Beck	man	I	must	go	home	

It is important that the student have something new set before him at each lesson. Spend about one-third of the second lesson reviewing and practicing Chapter Nine. The teacher might then read aloud Chapter Four, The Foundation of Good English Diction. Invite the pupil to ask questions and be sure that every paragraph is clearly understood. This will lead very naturally to the blocked-out examples on pages 29-32.

I often introduce the subject and practice of diction by asking my pupil to repeat after me the words "actors and actresses." Almost

---

[2] See page 61, 3rd line from bottom through line 14, page 62, page 63, all of paragraph 2.

invariably, the sound of K (which should follow the first letter, A2, of each noun) is entirely omitted by him, and in its place he has a closed throat. Then I imitate *his* speech, speaking close to his ear. Finally I speak the phrase correctly. Perhaps my pupil hears the difference, perhaps not. I continue to speak it over and over again, first wrongly, then correctly.

At this point it is well to block out the little phrase in pencil. Get the pupil to tell you what to write down. What does the phrase *sound like* when we strip it of all its consonants? What is the "vowel skeleton?" I illustrate by speaking one or two, perhaps all six vowels, as follows: A2 A3 A2 A2 E E.

Now, let us find out what "bundles" (consonants) these "people" (vowels) are carrying. A2 seems to be quite alone, but ktA3 seem to want to go together. I repeat the sound of "ktA3" many times, then "A2 ktA3," until the student begins to realize *how* he must listen. When this has once happened, all is smooth sailing, and the entire phrase presently is completed: A2 ktA3 rzA2 ndA2 ktrE sE z. Many people have difficulty with the final consonant sound, Z. They do not realize they are pronouncing it "s." This is because they end the phrase by resting in the form of the consonant s instead of breathing into the *form* of the preceding vowel E. When this short phrase has been mastered, the student is ready to complete it as on page 30:

```
Actors      and    actresses      ought    to
A2 ktA3   rzA2 ndA2 ktrE sE      zA3      ttU

  articulate      distinctly
A rtĬ kiU lE    itdĬ stĬ n͡gktlĬ
```

After the remaining examples on pages 29-32 have been studied and spoken, anything at all in the line of diction may be attempted. (See page 159.)

Speak each syllable very slowly, and be sure you hear the vowel and its accompanying consonant or consonant cluster *spoken as a unit;* be certain that you do not utter the consonant or cluster first, then the vowel directly after. This wrong use of the head mechanism is frequently the result of an earnest desire to be understood; hence the speaker or singer *emphasizes the consonants.* But this action defeats our purpose (clear diction) instead of furthering it; for it closes the throat with a spasm, and makes speaking and singing difficult. On the other hand, if *all* consonants as well as vowels are spoken and sung *on the breath,*[3] you will begin to hear truly and the head mechanism will function normally. All good traits have a tendency to hang together. The same is true of bad traits. *Consistency,* whether for weal or for woe, is a law of our physical being.

Many Americans have an unfortunate habit of closing and almost fixing the jaw when they speak. This makes them appear to talk through their teeth. The result is misery from every standpoint. Of course the reason is deep-seated. An unrelaxed condition prevails throughout the *entire* body because the mind is unrelaxed, tense, and hurried. *Where* do we set up right or wrong conditions of feeling and listening — conditions that result either in noble, expressive speech and song, or the contrary? The answer is brief and simple: *in the mind.*

Many years ago I had a pupil who was a gifted singer as well as a competent, inspiring teacher. She taught voice in a local high school, and she thought her students might find it interesting if I paid them a visit and talked a little about singing. The idea intrigued me, and as the appointed day approached, I began to consider just what I should say. This was a new experience for me, and it was a trifle alarming to be told that I must limit my talk to exactly fifteen minutes!

I felt that it was important to give those young people a comprehensive view of the subject *as a whole,*[4] and that I must make myself unmistakably clear. I began to question my own adequacy. I was sure of my ground, but how in the world could I tell my story in fifteen relentless minutes? It was helpful to know that the high-school

[3] See Chapter 8, "The Escalator."
[4] See pages 99-100.

young people had already been conditioned to my point of view regarding singing — that they understood what it meant to reason from causes to effects.

The night before the proposed visit a sudden inspiration struck me with the inevitableness of a round ball dropping into a round hole, and my problem was solved. Next morning I fared forth with courage and enthusiasm.

"I want to talk to you about the setting up of right conditions for singing," I began, standing, chalk in hand, before a blank blackboard. "First of all, *where* do we set up these conditions? *In the mind!*"

As I talked I drew a large circle, labeling it "Mind," within which I constructed two smaller spheres which I marked "Feeling" and "Hearing." Out from Feeling branched two more circles — "Relaxation" and "Power"; from Hearing, also two circles — "Pure Vowels" and "Accurate Pitch."

"Now," I went on, "these last four circles in a row re-unite to bring about marvelous results:

Relaxation plus Power equals 'Singing on the Breath.'

Accurate Pitch plus Pure Vowels equals 'Resonance.'

"These two circles symbolize the two elements which, when unrestricted, *ungoverned*, yet *recognized* by us, unite in the final great circle:

BALANCE OF RESONANCE AND BREATH[5]

"Every desired effect in speaking and singing (foremost among which are tonal beauty and flawless diction) is included in the Balance of Breath and Resonance. When we have a speaking and singing instrument in which this Balance prevails, we have 'great natural voice expression'[6] — a medium capable of carrying every human emotion."

---

[5] See pages 82 and 56, last paragraph.
[6] See page 83.

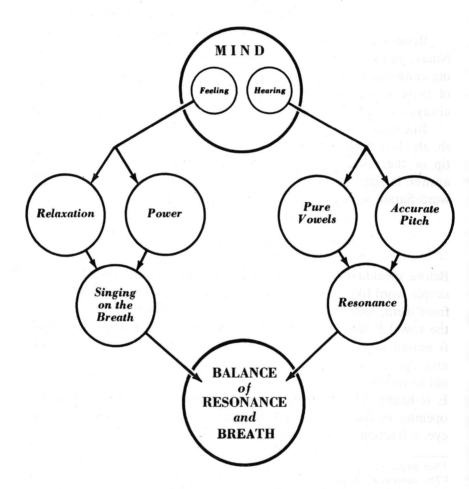

LESSON III

Besides using the consonants f, n, l (given as examples in Chapter Nine), you will have found these exercises equally easy if the following consonants were substituted: m, b, p, v, d, t, k, g, ng, th.[1] None of these sounds disturbs the position of the *tip of the tongue* — always *out*, covering the lower front teeth and touching the lower lip.[2]

But what about other consonant sounds? What about s, z, j, r, ch, sh, zh? It is impossible to pronounce these sounds clearly without the tip of the tongue going *back*, behind the lower front teeth. The answer is simpler than might be supposed. Take, for instance, the word Sarah, which would be blocked so:

S a r a h

sE   rA4

Before speaking it, set up the same conditions you would for a very simple word like "lama" — jaw hanging, tongue lying out over lower front teeth, touching lip. Now *hear* the first syllable being spoken — the vowel E with its consonant s. The jaw *is lifted* while the tongue *is moved away by the ear* to the exact spot necessary for the clear articulation of the consonant s. Immediately after, the tongue flops out to its normal position, the jaw drops open slightly, and the vowel E is heard. This in-and-out action of the tongue and closing-and-opening of the jaw happen simultaneously, in the twinkling of an eye, a fraction of a second.[3]

---

[1] See pages 66-67.
[2] The consonants n, d, and t are pronounced *in English* with the tongue tip back of the roots of the upper front teeth. At the moment, however, we are dealing with *Italian* vowels and consonants.
[3] See page 62.

The same actions occur when you pronounce the second syllable, rA4. Mouth, tongue, and jaw stay in the E position until the ear *hears* the second syllable; the jaw *is lifted* thereby and the tongue *is moved* to the exact spot necessary for the articulation of the consonant r (rolled or not); then the tongue flops out again and the jaw drops open as the vowel A4 is heard.[4]

Words containing the consonant sounds z, j, ch, sh, zh will seem no more complicated than the word Sarah. Always remember that the tongue should stay *out,* touching the lower lip. Then *hear* all consonants and consonant clusters *very clearly. Never emphasize or dwell in any consonant form* — not even in n, m, ng. Make light of them and *slip through* them instantaneously (and apparently carelessly!)[5] to the following vowel sound, in whose form you should dwell until *hearing the next syllable* moves you on to new forms, or until the breath has been inhaled.[6]

In English poetry we sometimes come across amazing consonant clusters. One such occurs in the first line of the charming old love song by Purcell, "I attempt from love's sickness to fly":

```
I   attempt    from   love's   sickness   to   fly   etc.
A  iA2  tE   mptfrA4  mlA4     vzsĭ  knE   stU   flA  i
```

mptfr! What a cluster! Most singers swallow at least one of the three middle consonants. But we must not fail to demonstrate the truth that no consonant or consonant cluster has power to dam up the flow of the breath stream, the perpetually moving medium that carries all human sounds throughout our life.[7] Every one of these five consonants must be uttered, the three unvoiced (asperated) ones, p t f, as well as the voiced ones m and r. This utterance will take

---

[4] See page 66, line 3. See also pages 87 and 88.
[5] See page 85, paragraph 2.
[6] See page 63, paragraph 2.
[7] See all of Chapter 8, especially page 58, paragraph 2.

care of itself if (while keeping right conditions) we permit these five sounds to ride comfortably on the breath stream, accompanied by a heavy, loosely flopping jaw and the *ever exacting ear*, which really governs every mechanical activity of our instrument.

The tongue is by nature the most pliable organ in the body. If we keep right conditions of feeling and hearing, it will perform its task of uttering consonants without our *direction*. If we insist upon "bossing the job" or trying conscientiously to help at all, trouble begins. And we certainly have enough to keep us busy, setting up and maintaining those right conditions![8]

By the third lesson you will be ready for a new speech drill. Up to this time you have practiced only on syllables that change consonants while keeping the same vowel: fa-na-la, fe-ne-le, etc. Here is an exercise that retains the consonant while the vowel changes. Symbols for mouth positions are: Laugh A , Pout E&I , Smile O , Whistle U[9].

This exercise presents no difficulties to the mind. But it does take patience to train the body-machine. Do not expect to master the entire exercise at once. Instead, begin with the first three syllables

---

[8] After working according to these ideas for a few weeks, one young woman remarked: "Now I can see how mistaken I have been. I have always believed in 'easy singing.' I thought if I worked hard enough and long enough, I would one day be able to sing *really easily*. Now I realize *easy singing* is not a *goal* to be attained finally, but a *path* which one must tread from the very beginning, from the very first lesson. Without hurry or worry, this 'easy path' leads surely to its goal — beautiful, noble singing, which is the heart's desire." Ida Auer-Herbeck called that goal "great natural voice expression."

[9] Never *tighten* the lips when speaking or singing U. The sound passes through a *relaxed* whistling form, as relaxed as possible.

of the second measure: bO bU bA. Go through them twice on one breath, ending with an inhalation at *. Repeat as many times as you please without breaking the rhythm.

Use a hand mirror. Be very sure that jaw, mouth, and tongue tumble rhythmically and spontaneously from one vowel form to the next. End the little phrase by breathing into the final vowel form at bA.

It will help greatly to form the right habit if you *speak the mouth positions rhythmically* a few times, thus:

Now practice the syllables above, and you will find that the right positions come along without your giving them a thought.

Apply the same method to the first measure, then unite it with the second. Almost without realizing it, you will find your head-machine tumbling through the first half of the exercise.

The last half presents no real difficulty, except perhaps the first two syllables, the first of which (bA) is uttered as rapidly as possible. This is easily accomplished if your machine (jaw - tongue - lips) remains *heavy* (relaxed).[10] At this point you will find it useful to "speak the positions" of the complete exercise rhythmically:

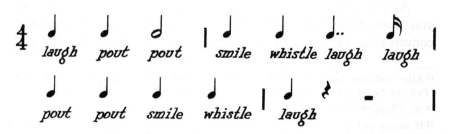

---

[10] See page 62, line 2.

The foregoing exercise may be practiced *staccato* to great advantage:

bIA bIE bII   bIO bIU bIA   bIA bIE bII bIO bIU bIA

Perform this staccato exercise with marching precision and spirit. *Be sure* the jaw remains hanging in every vowel position. *Do not* anticipate the next consonant! *Do not move* until your hearing and the rhythm compel you to do so![11]
Note: The only *legato* spot occurs when passing from bIA to bIE, end of second measure.

Go through the alphabet, using the following consonants with the five vowels: b, d, f, g, j, k, l, m, n, p, r, s, t, v, z. The consonant clusters on page 67 are especially useful, though some are difficult. Bear in mind that none of them has power to *keep* the tongue back of the teeth after you speak it!

My teacher, Ida Auer-Herbeck, used to say: "If you can sing German, that most difficult of tongues, as Italian *should* be sung, then all other languages will be child's play to you." Of course she was right. Our task is to convert into Italian, as it were, every language (including our own English) in which we may elect to speak or sing.[12]

As you acquire it, try to apply this speech principle to anything you speak or read aloud, as well as to ordinary daily talk. A telephone conversation affords an ideal opportunity for unobserved practice![13]

---

[11] After studying voice for several months, a student made a significant discovery: "I've just found out that you open your mouth *under your ears, not* with your *lips!*"
[12] See Chapters 4 through 7.
[13] If actors and actresses will practice the simple exercises suggested, they will be rewarded by finding the freedom that enables them to realize more completely whatever role they may study.

Young singers should never abandon these initial speech exercises. Five minutes of daily work on them as well as the application of the same *principle* to the text of all arias and songs will simplify whatever singing problems may arise. "Sing as you speak" — **yes,** *if* your speaking is right!

LESSONS IV AND V

A review of the First, Second and Third Lessons, with much time given to blocking and speaking the quotations to be found on pages 159 to 166.

It is impossible to estimate how long it will take a student to master the foregoing exercises. If the teacher has impressed him with their *importance* and if he has naturally good physical coordination, sensitivity, and the ability to concentrate, then the time may be greatly shortened. What we are seeking seems so tiny, so *trivial,* that I often liken it to "concentrating on fly specks." Whenever the mind becomes weary, a change of thought is necessary.

During this period (of approximately half a dozen lessons), I would suggest a division of the lesson time into three parts. Devote the first third to review; the middle third to new work; the last third to speech itself, reading quotations and blocking out a few of them. To that end, the list of quotations to be found on page 159 may be useful.

There is more than one way to reach an objective. In outlining my own procedure when presenting the first steps in the study of voice, I suggest it merely as *one* way to approach the problem. However, some definite plan of action, both consistent and flexible, must be in the mind of the teacher. No two pupils are exactly alike, and it is the teacher's business to fit the shoe to the foot.

The really good teacher is something of a psychologist. Instead of trying to graft his own ready-made ideas upon those of his pupil, he will *work from within.* He must first see everything — all of life —

from his pupil's standpoint. Then gradually and very gently he will begin to overcome the limitations he finds there. In the student's mind there must never be a moment of confusion. From the very first lesson every step of the way must be crystal clear. At first it may seem as though a black curtain hangs before his eyes. The first lesson makes a tiny pin-prick in the blackness, letting in a beam of light. Subsequent lessons plus the pupil's growth augment the pin-pricks rapidly, until the curtain has disappeared and all is light. The subject is then seen in its entirety.

We, my pupil and I, are like mural painters standing before a vacant wall upon which we begin to sketch, in proportion and very rapidly, the entire picture of *voice education.* When the wall has been covered with our bold, swift strokes, we begin to concentrate on filling in the details of our painting. We devote ourselves completely to component parts, one by one, *never forgetting the relation of each to the whole.* Standing back now and then, we view each developing detail in proper proportion.

Now, breathing,[1] diction,[2] and resonance, together with their many subdivisions, are the *definite parts* of the *whole great painting.* They are *results,* and we must never regard them as otherwise. In dealing with them, separately and collectively, we must use no trickery (disguised as "short cuts"); we must follow no "orders," no "recipes." To do so would be like throwing sand into machinery. Instead, we never stop setting up right conditions of *feeling and listening,* and so stay faithful to our *singing principle.* Only by working in some such fashion are we able to keep our clarity of vision — our vocal balance.

Fifty years ago there was a prosperous teacher in Dresden who emphasized "kleine Mund" (small mouth) as being *the* important idea in singing. If a singer would merely maintain throughout his

---

[1] See Chapters 9 and 10.
[2] See Chapters 4 through 7.

range "eine kleine Mund," most of his difficulties would vanish. The diction of this man's pupils was, I recall, one prolonged "OO," and their singing seemed uncomfortable, at least to an observer's eye and ear.

Another pedagogue declared the hands must be pressed tightly against each other for "support," and all would be well. Although such advice may seem on its very face devoid of sense, many concert singers today would seem to attest their faith in its supposed magic!

At the turn of the century, a furor was sweeping the singing world. The burden of its import was: "Project your tones 'dans la masque' if you wish to solve the problem of *resonance.*" The great singer who first made that remark failed to realize that he was dealing with a *result,* not a *cause.* It would have been more accurate to say: "If right conditions are once set up and then maintained during singing, the singer will experience a sensation of *resonance* (busy-ness), swirling unimpeded and *undirected by him* throughout the *entire head* — eyes, ears, nose, mouth, cranium — not merely 'dans la masque'." The question of *resonance* is indeed solvable, but only by recognizing it as *result,* and hence concerning ourselves *only* with its *cause.*

"Lower the larynx and raise the soft palate, and you will make an open throat and a round, rich tone" are specific orders and definite promises frequently expressed. Our business is strictly to set up and maintain right conditions for singing. This is carried on in the sphere of feeling and hearing — not of *doing.* Nature takes care of the realm of operation; but if we insist upon "running the machine," no room is left for nature's administration![3]

"Learn to 'color' the vowels, if you would have tonal beauty" is another recipe for "what to do." How can we color vowels and at the same time preserve their purity? The thirteen vowels plus their various combinations (see page 130) give us a rich mass of color

---

[3] See all of Chapter 2.

with which to paint our song pictures. Whatever is used comes spontaneously, through the *freed emotions,* however, not from the singer's clever calculations.

A prominent New York voice teacher and coach says: "You must 'megaphone' tones if you would have them powerful. Support from the diaphragm! Good diction is a matter of the correct management of the lips, the tongue, and the teeth!" etc. etc. Certainly a complicated set of directions for *managing* the singing instrument!

These rare bits of advice are stones offered to hungry young people crying for bread. They are orders the student is supposed to carry out.[4] If these teachers had had a larger, over-all view of the subject, they would have dropped their over-emphasis on relatively small details which concern *results* and do not go back to *causes.*[5]

---

[4] See page 19.
[5] See page 20.

LESSONS VI AND VII

The new work which may now be started takes us to the piano. Here we add musical pitches to the speaking exercises already practiced, as we "talk" the same syllables *staccato* on the first five tones of the scale of C major:

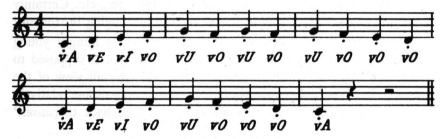

vA vE vI vo vU vo vU vo vU vo vo vo

vA vE vI vo vU vo vo vo vA

It is enough to practice the first half until it goes well before adding the last half. Transpose the little exercise down into the key of B, then into B-flat, then A. Now begin a new series with a new consonant (or cluster) in the key of D-flat; transpose down to C, then to B, then B-flat.[6] Begin again in the key of D, proceeding to D-flat, C, B. Lastly, begin on E-flat, continuing down to A and even to F, if you like. Change the consonant each time you begin a new series.

When the foregoing exercise has been fairly well mastered, expand it into the following one of similar rhythm:

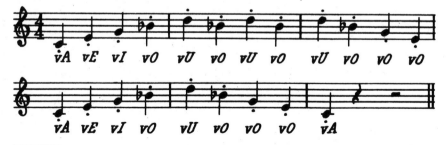

vA vE vI vo vU vo vU vo vU vo vo vo

vA vE vI vo vU vo vo vo vA

---

[6] Change these exercises occasionally to the minor mode, to rest the mind.

Talk the syllables on the various pitches, and proceed downward on semitones as in the previous exercise. The lowest tone should be about G below the staff, and the highest about E fourth space.

These two exercises are far from easy, and you should be neither impatient nor discouraged if it takes several lessons to master them.

LESSON VIII

Our first exercises (see Chapter Nine) maintained the vowel while the consonant changed. The next spoken exercises (see page 95) maintained the consonant while the vowel changed. The following exercises change both vowel and consonant with each utterance:

bE dA mE nI pO tU lA

This chain of Italian syllables has come down to us from the venerable Italian masters, and it affords a useful medium for the creation of innumerable exercises. It is the stepping stone to text, for, having gone through a thorough drilling in it both in speaking and singing,[1] you are well prepared to attempt simple songs.

This series of sounds may *look* plain enough on paper; but tumbling from one vowel-and-consonant form to the next is no easy matter. It is one of the very important details in our "mural painting" and is one result of having set up right conditions of *feeling and listening.*

Take the first two syllables, bE dA; speak them in a steady stream many times, noting the mouth positions their vowels bring (pout . . . laugh):

bE dA bE dA bE dA bE dA

Work out the next pair in the same way (laugh . . . pout):

dA mE dA mE dA mE

---

[1] See page 131.

and the next (pout . . . pout):
        mE   nI   mE   nI   mE   nI   mE   nI

and the next (pout . . . smile):
        nI   pO   nI   pO   nI   pO   nI   pO

and the next (smile . . . whistle):
        pO   tU   pO   tU   pO   tU   pO   tU

and finally the last pair (whistle . . . laugh):
        tU   lA   tU   lA   tU   lA   tu   lA.

Do not allow one single position to escape without your checking it.
Use your hand mirror and speak in a steady, unbroken stream, moving up and down the range of the voice. When you come to an ending, be certain to breathe into the form of the final vowel.[2]

Always speak these syllables in proper succession — clockwise —
and build similar exercises, using three syllables:

bE dA mE; dA mE nI; mE nI pO; nI pO tU; pO tU lA; etc. etc.

In like manner four syllables:

bE dA mE nI; dA mE nI pO; mE nI pO tU; nI pO tU lA; etc.

Then five, six, and finally seven:

        bE   dA   mE   nI   pO   tU   lA

Starting with the second syllable, dA, speak all seven, ending with
bE; then start on mE, ending with dA, etc. etc.

When the mouth positions begin to come of themselves, you will
find it amusing to vary the speed and the rhythm. For instance:

---

[2] See page 63, paragraph 2.

From the beginning the pupil should be urged to use his imagination to create all manner of interesting exercises, the more complicated the better.[3] What one does matters less than how one does it.

---

[3] When the student has begun to sing scales on *all* vowels, the above exercises will be useful put to music. See page 131.

LESSON IX

Even though the preceding exercises may be far from perfect by the third or fourth week, there is no reason why the student should not begin to study *staccato* and *legato* scales. In preparation we read together Chapter Eleven, The Mouth Positions.

The scale on the vowel A is the first and most important one to be studied.[1] The student will use the key suited to his type of voice; middle voices commence on A, lowest voices on G. The plan works out as follows for high voices:

Go over these first seven tones of the scale[2] two or three times, finally

---

[1] See pages 61 and 76-77.

[2] Symbols for alteration of mouth positions in ascending and descending scale passages:

ASCENDING

DESCENDING

ending with a coda. (This coda has the effect of keeping the singer's body alert at the *end* of the phrase.) You then breathe into the form of the last vowel uttered, and find yourself ready for the next phrase, should there be one.[3]

During the *staccato* scale passage you are seated. Now, your jaw hanging loosely, you rise from the chair,[4] inhaling as you do so. Immediately repeat the exercise, this time *legato,* ending as before with the lively little *staccato* coda:

Rhythmic breathing[5] should be applied to the above exercises as well as to those that follow:

SING THREE TIMES THROUGH, END WITH CODA, BREATHE INTO THE FORM. Repeat this routine many times, never losing the rhythm. A *rhythm of the breath* (intake. . .outgo. . .intake. . .outgo. . .intake . . .outgo etc.) now becomes apparent to the singer, and suggests the slow, regular swinging of a pendulum.

Some pupils have compared *rhythmic breathing* to breathing while swimming. It is of *great value* in developing natural, "deep" breathing.[6] As you practice these scale exercises, you will *hear* and *feel* your voice improve with every repetition. It will grow smoother, more accurate; the vowel pronunciation will remain true throughout, and the back of the throat will stay placid and changeless; the entire body

---

[3] See page 63, paragraph 2.
[4] See pages 9 ,17, 70.
[5] See page 73.
[6] See page 72.

will feel as though it were taking part in this activity, even though you stand quietly, with tranquil, relaxed hands.

Repeat this entire performance, starting on the third degree of the scale (D)—middle voices on C#, lowest voices on B—first *staccato,* then *legato,* applying "rhythmic breathing" as above:

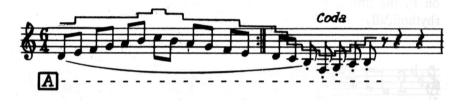

In this manner you have built up the nine-note scale, which you now proceed to practice as follows, not forgetting "rhythmic breathing":

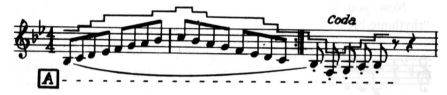

LESSON X

By the next lesson you should be ready to add another seven-note figure to the nine-note scale on A, G, or B-flat. This third group begins on F, the fifth degree of the scale of B-flat. Remember to breathe rhythmically:

Now you have built a "double scale," which (not forgetting "rhythmic breathing") proceeds like this:

The scale on B-flat (A, or G) may be further developed by gradually adding two more seven-note figures to the "double scale." Start on A (2nd space); this will give you a "triple scale." Finally, starting on C (3rd space) you will have a "quadruple scale," extending to B♭ (2nd added space).

111

Be quite certain that the mouth positions are as strictly observed as are the fingers of a pianist who practices scales. Unless he disciplines his fingers and insists upon *always* playing scales and arpeggios correctly, he can never hope to perform really well, no matter how musical he may be. Nor should you, the singer, avoid a similar discipline with respect to mouth positions. Your reward will not be long in coming. Within a few months' time, a year at the latest, you will find your loose jaw and mouth *naturally seeking* the right positions, just because your voice *feels* and *sounds* best to you if you observe them.

Always make use of rhythmic breathing when practicing scales. A metronome is a great help in preventing you from slackening the time. It is almost indispensable in the study of arpeggios and trills, as well as scales. It stimulates one both physically and mentally.

You may sit at the piano and play along with the *staccato* practice, though the use of a pitch pipe for the initial tone really provides for a keener development of the ear than the use of the piano with every *staccato* tone. When practicing *legato, never* play the piano—and *always* stand.

A seven-note section of a *staccato* scale is like a small blueprint. It plots the pattern for the singing of the *legato* scale to follow. If there are any discrepancies in pitch or vowel pronunciation, they are easily detected when singing the *staccato* scale. Should this short succession of tones call for a change of mouth position, that mechanical adjustment can be accomplished easier and the right habit trained more definitely if scales are first practiced *staccato.*

The tones of a *staccato* scale are like separate, precisely matched beads. A *legato* scale is these very same beads strung on the continuous *breath stream.* Scales should be sung absolutely unemotionally, without overaccenting the natural rhythmical beats. The great purpose of scale practice is the equalization of the voice.

So far, nothing has been said concerning *dynamics.* The student, it is assumed, has been singing the foregoing scales in "normal" voice

—that is to say, in neither his loudest nor his softest voice. What, if anything, happens when these scales are sung *pianissimo?*

When singing A, the only change that takes place is in the mouth positions; and that is merely a difference in *degree of opening.* The general form of the mouth is more closed and even more smiling than when singing normally; but the changes in mouth position take place just as promptly and precisely when ascending and descending scales. *Pianissimo* scales are exactly like normally sung scales in miniature, as it were.

Pianissimo never means weak, powerless, lacking in character. It is just as potent, dramatically, as *fortissimo,* and demands fully as much from the entire human instrument as do the loudest tones.[7]

Most students, particularly those who have had previous training of a wrong kind, tend to make a crescendo towards the top of an ascending scale passage,[8] accenting the highest note especially. As such a singer descends the scale, a number of related changes take place:

His body falls, sinks in. It is like a car coasting down hill without power. The shape of the throat changes, sometimes violently, so that a listener hears a "break" or a "click" at one or more definite spots. At the same time, true vowel pronunciation and resonance are lost. Finally, after the tonic or starting tone is reached, only a shallow breath can be inhaled by the exhausted singer.

A cure must be found for such vocal misbehavior, which is more general than might be supposed. The remedy, applicable to the singing of *all* vowels, may be found on page 120, paragraph 2, and on page 121.

The student (and the teacher too) should not expect the begin-

---

[7] See page 143.
[8] If while singing a beginner can be persuaded to *accent the floor* with his *pushing feet* (heels included), the compulsion to accent the top tone will cease to trouble him.

ner's voice to be *beautiful*. Because his first new sounds are *right* does not mean they will be more beautiful than a baby's or an animal's. But it is upon this foundation of *natural sound* that genuine beauty builds itself. In fact, the whole process of right singing is like discovering an individual's *real* voice, his *child voice,* as it was before it was cluttered with the tensions and sophistications of adulthood. And only when his *child voice* has become freed can his beautiful adult voice come to fruition.

Of all vowels, A seems to be the most troublesome, especially for Americans.[9] The battle, however, is entirely a mental one the student fights with himself. When he has won this particular victory, he has found the ultimate key to "easy singing."

The *right,* bright sound of A seems at first so strange, so childish, so downright *ugly* to the beginner that he is apt to shrink from *allowing* such a horrid noise to come through unaltered. Surreptitiously, almost unconsciously, he tries to better it. In so doing, *he changes both the vowel pronunciation and the shape of the back of the throat.* This results in sudden loss of resonance, immediate curtailment of range, and general discomfort.

A pupil who came to me with a dark, throaty voice fought the bright, "silly" pronunciation of A for some time. When she finally permitted it to come through unchallenged, she exclaimed, "Oh, that *nasty* little A!" At the same time, she had to admit it did not *hurt* her, that she *felt* quite comfortable and "throatless" when she let it remain throughout the scale.

From that moment she began to develop "new ears" and to trust them. If her old ears had been really dependable, she argued, would she not have made herself into a great singer without anyone's help? She began to like "nasty little A." It never deceived her. When combined with right conditions of activity *below* the collar bones,[10]

---

[9] See page 61, 3rd paragraph.
[10] See Chapter 10.

her once unpleasant voice became appealing and beautiful in quality. "Nasty little A" is like the Beast in the old fairy tale "Beauty and the Beast." Though hideous in appearance, he was so gentle and kind that he won Beauty's compassion and finally her love. When she took him to her heart, he was instantly transformed into a radiant prince! Once accepted, "nasty little A" reveals itself as *resonance*. It is not the end of vocal beauty but it is assuredly the beginning, the seed. Without it, the voice is without life or charm, uninteresting to hear, and a labor to produce.

I have often compared this resonance to violin playing. If you are very close to a violinist, you will hear a noise quite extraneous to the musical sound coming from his instrument. It is the scraping of the horsehair upon the catgut. A few feet away, this noise, unpleasant in itself, is not discernible. It is like nasty A, very apparent to the singer himself (because of the close proximity of larynx and ear) but transformed into resonance and beauty to the ears of a listener only a short distance away.

People who sing really well are those who have found the magic combination of *hearing* and *feeling, resonance plus singing on the breath,* which together constitute the heart's desire, vocally.[11] These fortunate people often try to describe their sensations when they realize they are singing their best. Almost always these descriptions take a pictorial form.

Elizabeth Rethberg once told an interviewer that, to her, right singing was "like a silver ball playing in a fountain," the silver ball (resonance) playing with the upward moving stream of water (the breath stream). This is a perfect description of "the balance of resonance and breath"—of *motion.*[12]

Ida Auer-Herbeck called this resonance "der Kern im Ton" (the kernel, core, of the tone). She also likened it and its resulting vibra-

---

[11] See page 58; also see pages 91 and 92.
[12] See page 56; page 82, paragraph 3.

tions to a pebble dropped into a pool of still water. From that little center the wavelets go forth in ever widening circles which she compared to "die Wirbeln im Ton" (the swirl in the tone), the overtones and undertones, the "ring."

J. C. Cooper called this quality "the *ping* in the tone." When he heard such a quality in a voice, it was, he said, as though a bright light suddenly shone high up in a corner of his studio. He called this "light" his "guide."

I am dealing at considerable length with the vowel A because it is the *key vowel*. When it feels and sounds as it should to the student, then resonance and breath are in balance. He finds that the other pure vowels, E, I, O, U, fall into line with little difficulty when their turn comes. Following A, they too tend to keep the same balance of breath and resonance.

When you discover the correct mouth positions for the remaining four vowels,[13] when you *hear the same vowel pronunciation* throughout your range, when you once experience the *feelinglessness* of an *unchanging throat* while singing them, then each vowel will match in quality the resonance you discovered when you allowed "nasty little A" to pass through unaltered.

Each vowel possesses its own identity quite distinct from that of the others. At the same time, they all share a basic quality. I like to compare the five pure vowels A E I O U (as spoken in Italian) to five children who have the same parents. One child has blue eyes and blond hair; another, black eyes and hair; a third, grey eyes and black hair; another, red hair and green eyes; and a fifth, brown eyes and hair. They are quite unlike in appearance, yet *all have the same origin*.

What I have just said about "nasty little A" and its connotations of "childishness," "silliness," "brightness," etc., ties in with what I term "the child voice." The child-voice idea, which stems straight

---

[13] See Chapter 11.

from *feeling* and *hearing,* should be made use of in the training of *all* voice types, from the lowest bass to the highest soprano.

All very young creatures, lambs, calves, and babies for instance, are born with voices that "carry," that cut through the air far more keenly and surely than do the voices of their elders. All these young things utter their primitive calls on a noise approaching A2,[14] "nasty little A" carried to an extreme. Even though this piercing, brash sound becomes somewhat modified with time, enough of it remains for us to agree that the voices of children carry better and sound easier than do the voices of most grownups.

Upon reaching maturity, a sudden change in the voice becomes apparent, less so with most girls, because the locale of their range undergoes no transition. Boys' voices, on the other hand, shift downward an octave.

During this metamorphosis much mischief is often wrought, especially in the case of baritones and basses. In my opinion, older people are often to blame for this. They are apt to ridicule, thoughtlessly, the peculiar sounds of the early adolescent male. A boy sometimes begins a sentence with his newly acquired "man's voice" only to end it like a child. To a sensitive lad of fourteen the grown-up laughter that usually follows is often embarrassing. To avoid it, he "grabs" the new, deep, low voice and tries to *fix* it permanently, thereby stiffening larynx and throat and causing much physical damage.

He now has two voices at war with each other. When he attempts to sing, this strife is even more evident. Naturally, he likes the rich, manly voice better. But its upper range is limited. Strive as he will, if he is a baritone, he cannot *make* it ascend further than D♭ or D (2nd space above F-clef staff). If he tries to drive it higher, the back of his throat changes shape with sudden violence and he finds himself singing with the old child voice, which will run on with perfect ease for almost another octave. Now, unless these two voices can resolve

---
[14] See page 24.

their difficulties and become friendly, unless we can find a way to weld them into one solid piece, the human instrument remains divided, broken, like the pieces of Siegfried's sword.

By chance I once met a singing teacher whose graphic description of the essential voice-welding process struck me as being both unique and sound. Frank Carroll Giffin was the man who so generously shared with me this excellent fruit of his imaginative mind. That casual meeting was significant for me, and I enjoy passing on its import to others.

We were talking about the teaching of voice, particularly the male voice, and the necessity of *reconciling* the child voice with the one a boy acquires at puberty. His illustration was simple and direct:

"Here is the little boy's voice," said he, indicating horizontally the distance from fingertips to elbow of his right arm, "and here is the man's voice," placing his left arm similarly, the fingertips of both hands opposite but not touching. "Now," he went on, "these two voices are apt to fight each other until the young man begins to realize that they *must* become friendly. This can happen only when the child voice goes all the way down to the very lowest tone of the man's range" (here he touched the left elbow with the tips of the right-hand fingers) "and sings every single tone along with the man's voice!" His forearms were now a unit, fingers to elbows. "In this way the 'two voices' become one, and proceed easily and without a 'break' throughout a long range."

By means of this union of the two voices, the depth, roundness, and richness of the man's becomes one with the brilliance, fleetness, and ease of the child's—the somber, heavy element with the carrying factor. Then indeed, every tone will be both bright and dark—in balance.

In encouraging a student to *allow* the child voice to roam freely up and down the entire range, I suggest to him never to try to "get" the lowest pitches, thereby changing the shape of the throat. Instead, I recommend his merely *talking* them on pitch, childishly, no matter how weak they may seem to him. The weakness is only a transition stage. The ultimate outcome will be far greater than before in power, beauty, and ease, and a more extensive low range will result. While he is singing, I speak constantly of how *silly* his voice is sounding *to him*—how infantile, foolish, childish—even "no good." I sing this unwanted, unpleasant sound close to his ear, for (the ear being very near the larynx) his own voice will sound to him like mine. It is often easier to learn from imitation than from discourse, and he is reassured when he notices that my voice sounds better at a short distance.

Although the change from a little girl's voice to that of a grown woman is less noticeable to others than the change through which boys' voices go, the identical metamorphosis occurs. In contraltos (rarest of all voices) the change parallels that of basses. If the individual has discarded the child's voice, there will be a mental as well as a physical fixation about the upper range, which will reach barely to C (3rd space, G-clef) and sometimes not farther than A (2nd space). Below that the voice is strong and heavy, and will in time become mannish in quality. But when the child voice has been restored to its rightful use, a transformation immediately begins. Within a few weeks an upper range becomes manifest, the voice begins to flow naturally, and resonance and breath seek a balance. The door to freedom has been flung open wide!

One point must be made very clear to the reader. The "child voice" and the so-called "falsetto" are not at all the same thing. Falsetto, as its name implies, is a *false voice*. It is destructive and its persistent use will ultimately ruin a singer. The child voice, on the contrary, is the most important and valuable factor in the training of *all* singers, especially men. Opposing characteristics of these two are interesting. Whereas the child voice may swell and diminish at will, the breathy, non-resonant falsetto refuses to alter dynamically.

As soon as you can demonstrate that you have thoroughly understood the foregoing explanation of the child voice, particularly with reference to the vowel A, you are ready to master the remaining fundamental Italian vowels. You will experience little difficulty if you permit the child voice to sing them for you.

LESSON XI

THE VOWEL E (PRONOUNCED AS IN HEAD, FED)[1]

For many Americans, the true pronunciation of this vowel is not easy to maintain throughout a scale. We start out bravely enough, say on B (2nd added space below staff, G-clef),with what we *think* is the sound of E, only to find it gliding through various changes of pronunciation quite unintentional on our part. This is especially noticeable when we descend the scale to the speaking area. If we listen with keen concentration we may hear ourselves producing a sound resembling O,[2] perhaps mixed with A4.[3] Pure E has faded away. Why should this be so, and how can it be corrected?[4]

An unintentional change in vowel pronunciation always denotes a change in the shape of the back of the throat. When the ear asks for a pure vowel, the machine *above* the collar bones spontaneously coordinates to that end, *if* right conditions of feeling *below* the collar bones are being maintained.[5] But if such is not the case, if the under body fails to do its duty, then the throat is powerless to coordinate naturally. It is as though there were sand in its machinery, forcing it to coordinate *unnaturally*. Actual and painful strife ensues in that region, resulting in a vowel distorted almost beyond recognition.

An imaginary conversation between the parts of the body most vital to singing might run like this:

---

[1] See page 63, paragraph 3; also Chapter 11, page 78.
[2] See Chapter 5, page 35.
[3] See Chapter 4, page 24.
[4] See page 113.
[5] See pages 15, 17, 18.

THE EAR (who is really King of All): I insist upon hearing *pure E, no variations!*

THE THROAT: King Ear refuses to tolerate a change in pronunciation of the vowel E? Then, as the singing proceeds, I must not alter my form in the slightest degree! Instead, I must remain placidly sleeping!

THE BODY (below the collar bones): What? The Throat refuses to change its shape? Then I dare not be lazy! *I must continue to support everything above me!* For I am really the slave, and King Ear is the Master![6]

If you can manage to sing a scale while you are at the same time performing the "chair exercise" you will hit upon that magic combination of *feeling and hearing* which is at the root of all that is beautiful, right, and desirable in singing.

In the search for the pure vowel E, curious manifestations in the way of feeling and hearing make their appearance. "Can *this* be right, this primitive, animal-like sound coming through me?" the beginner questions, hesitating to accept it. "Is this feeling of utterly *crude* resonance right? It makes my head swim and I feel almost dizzy! Ought I not to *tone it down* some?"

To these questions there is just one answer: "Yes! Both your hearing and feeling are *right!* Never interfere with *results!* They are Nature's business. Ours is *only* to *set up and then maintain* right conditions of feeling and listening. Even the dizzy sensation is right, an encouraging, temporary symptom. In a few days the head will have grown accustomed to this acute, new resonance. *Never* 'tone it down'!"

The only way to beautify the voice is to use a deeper and deeper activity of the coordinated torso and legs.[7] *Power* can manifest itself *only* in proportion to our *relaxation.*[8]

---

[6] See Chapter 10 in toto, and especially pages 70-71.
[7] See Chapter 10.
[8] See page 18.

A remark made by a high school lad was both amusing and true. When at last he allowed pure, crude, unalloyed E to pass through his voice machine, he burst into laughter at the resulting noise. "It sounds just like a calf in the low part and a sheep in the high!" was his vivid description.

"Did *you* try to *make* your voice sound that way?" I asked.

"No indeed!" he replied. "I'm just trying to pronounce pure E and nothing else all the time!"

"Well," said I, "perhaps Nature *intends* pure E to sound exactly that way to *you* when you are singing scales—like a calf in the low and a sheep in the high. To me, a few feet away, that was a beautiful scale, resonant and powerful and plastic. Moreover, you kept the integrity of the vowel!"

The boy found it hard to believe that his E scale had really been beautiful! To him it had seemed far from that. But at least he had sung pure E, homogeneous throughout. It *felt* so easy that it seemed as though he no longer possessed a throat. He had permitted the *child voice* to sing *through* him, and had discovered thereby the *resonance natural* to the vowel E!

Another pupil made a rare remark concerning the *feel* of his tongue when singing this vowel: "It seems as though it no longer belongs to me, as though someone had stuck it into my mouth!"

The path of a singer is one of endless discovery, revelation. When he attempts to describe these personal experiences, they naturally come forth pictorially, in similes (see pages 115 and 116); and these pictures invariably refer to feeling and hearing: "It sounds like—" or "It feels as though—" or "It seems as if—" etc.

The *natural resonance of E* (sounding much as though an animal were *singing through you*) matches the *natural resonance* you discovered in the vowel A—"nasty little A" to which you were at first so opposed.[9] Pure, resonant E, too, is Beauty's "Beast," and if you

---

[9] See page 114.

"take it to your heart" instead of evading it, you will be blessed a thousandfold.

The practice plan for E is the same as that employed for A. Note that (in the key of B) E does not alter the position of the mouth until the pitch C# (3rd space, G-clef) is reached.[10]

After the scale of B has been built up as far as the pitch E (4th space) in sections of seven tones,[11] the vowel E, double scale, may be practiced as follows:

E differs mechanically from all the other vowels. Both A and O cause the mouth to smile throughout the range. The mouth merely *opens by degrees, one* action, when the pitches begin to change its form. The vowel I maintains a pouty, closed mouth (a trifle less open than for E)[12] until the pitch D (4th line, G-clef) compels it to smile *but not to open* (again, *one* action). E, on the other hand, alters the mouth in *two ways.* Remaining rather closed and pouty up through B (3rd line, G-clef), it begins (in the key of B) *both* to hang open and to smile very slightly on the next tone, C# *(two actions).* This *double action* increases subtly as the scale proceeds upward. On descending the scale, this sequence is of course reversed; E causes the

---

[10] See page 78, paragraph 3.
[11] See page 108.
[12] See page 79.

mouth to *close and pout* very gradually until B (3rd line) is reached, at which point the smile has entirely disappeared and the mouth looks and feels as it did at the start, rather closed and pouty.

In the low and middle portion of the range, when the scale on the vowel E is sung *pianissimo,* it comes through a *closed, smiling mouth.* Very gradually and even more smilingly, the mouth is opened a trifle by each succeeding tone, commencing with C, third space.

LESSON XII

Many years ago I had a pupil with an extraordinary voice. She had found the vowel O particularly difficult to master, because she sang it through a "round hole" mouth. When, after many weeks of endeavor, she began to *feel* the right position for O and to *hear* its own peculiar resonance and pronunciation (Irish O), she exclaimed: *"Now* I know what Schipa meant!"

She then went on to tell me of having met and sung for the famous tenor, Tito Schipa. He had been enthusiastic in praising her beautiful voice, but he insisted there was something wrong about her singing of the vowel O. *He couldn't tell her what was the matter!* Being an Italian, with no need to think about it, he "sang as he spoke!"[2] During the entire evening he kept referring to the faulty vowel, saying, "Too bad about that O! Too bad about that O!"

When the student is learning how to sing, the experience of others is encouraging and of great value to him. A young girl with a beautiful coloratura soprano had some difficulty in hearing and feeling the right resonance for O. To my (outside) ears, her tone sounded breathy and hollow, like a flute instead of like a violin.

When she finally allowed the child voice to take over, her O at once became perfect, matching in quality her other pure vowels. She exclaimed delightedly: "It sounds *grainy,* doesn't it?" After that mo-

---

[1] See pages 64 and 79.
[2] See page 84, first paragraph.

ment of discovery, when the wrong old habit threatened, I needed merely to remind her that O sounded *grainy*. In making that remark, she had unwittingly presented me with a precious treasure, which I have been happy to pass on to other pupils. To her, "nasty little A," "animal-sounding E," and now "grainy-sounding O" were all in the same category, the same *vowel family*. No matter how varied their individual characteristics, they all had the same *resonance*, the same *parentage*. Since then, many a student has been encouraged to accept the "grainy sound" that the child voice brings to the vowel O.[3]

Here is a mechanical aid for sensing the correct O mouth positions: Hold an ordinary pencil lightly between the lips horizontally. Remove it without changing the contour of the mouth. The right position for O (middle and low portions of the range) will remain. From C (3rd space) on up, imagine that the pencil grows thicker at each semitone, as you allow the mouth to *hang into a fresh smile* with each ascending pitch.[4] To the singer, O sounds weaker than either A or E. *Never* try to make it strong!

If you imagine a still thinner pencil when singing O *pianissimo*, you will *feel instinctively* the right mouth openings, commencing on C, third space.

Practice O in the same manner as the two preceding vowels:[5]

Double scale

---

[3] See pages 79-80.
[4] See page 79.
[5] See pages 109 and 121.

LESSON XIII

The Vowel I (pronounced as in machine)[1]

Of all pure vowels, I strikes us as being the shrillest and sharpest. We almost feel compelled to "tone it down," to "improve" it. If we yield to this temptation in the slightest degree, out goes the resonance, the tongue grooves at the root and draws back from the lower front teeth, and we are suddenly and unpleasantly aware of the fact that we possess a throat.

If you pronounce *pure I* on every tone of the ascending scale, you will find that the tip of your heavy, relaxed tongue continues to remain out over the lower front teeth, while the thick of the tongue rises higher with each tone.

As was the case with the others, this vowel, too, will alter the contour of the mouth, but not until the pitch D (4th line) is reached. At this point, ever so slight a smile (merely a "twitch" of the corners of the mouth) appears, which increases with each semitone until, at the top of the scale, the smile is as broad as that of A, E, and O. The jaw, however, does not drop open.

While keeping right conditions of feeling and hearing, it is quite normal for the vowel I to cause the relaxed tongue to feel like a swollen thing, filling most of the throat and mouth. "How can the tone find space enough to come through?" you might ask incredulously. Nature works in mysterious ways. If you are *willing* to fall in line with her, all will be well. But if you argue *against* her, trouble

---

[1] See pages 63 and 79.

127

begins.[2] Let the thick, soft tongue ride high then, touching the upper back teeth, as it apparently wants to do.

The extreme shrillness of I is its own peculiar identity, its true characteristic—its contribution from the child voice. When balanced with the breath,[3] this ultra-shrillness turns at once into charming resonance, just as Beauty's Beast was transformed into a noble prince.[4] Ninety-nine parts breath-stream, and only one part I! But that one part must be absolutely *pure, shrill I!*

When I is sung *pianissimo,* the mouth smiles slightly through the low and middle tones, the smile increasing somewhat from D fourth line on higher.

Practice the scale of I in the same way you did the other vowels:[5]

Double scale

[2] See page 15, top of page.

[3] See page 57, lines 4-5.

[4] See page 115, first paragraph.

[5] See page 109.

LESSON XIV

The Vowel U (pronounced as in who)[1]

There is little more to be said about this vowel. Perhaps it is well to emphasize the fact that to you, the singer, it sounds ridiculously small and impotent—a "peep-squeak"—*if* you insist upon speaking a *pure vowel*. To the ears of other people, however, your U will seem to be quite adequate. (Note: Our English word "who" is a help in getting the correct pronunciation of U.)

Since there is practically no variation in lip formation, no change of mouth position while singing a scale on U,[2] it is not necessary to write out such a scale. I omit special practice on this vowel. I have found that, when the other four basic vowels are right—when they *match*—U follows along with them whenever we encounter it in a text.

Speaking of text, it is interesting and significant to note that, in all languages, U is the least frequently met of all vowel sounds, and the entire A family[3] appears most often.

The five basic, unaltered, pure vowels are like the three primary colors in the realm of painting—pure, crude red; pure, crude yellow; pure, crude blue. From various combinations of these three fundamental pigments, every subtle French shade is derived. In the realm of voice also, the peculiarities of our own English vowels as well as the (to our ears) strange vowel sounds indigenous to various nations —sounds so different from Italian—stem, nevertheless, straight from some combination of those clear, unmixed, fundamental Italian vowels.

---

[1] See pages 25, 65 and 80.
[2] Naturally, the mouth does not alter its position anywhere when U is sung *pianissimo*.
[3] See page 23.

129

In French, German, and English there are complex vowel sounds seemingly quite unrelated to the primal Italian vowels we have been isolating in our present study. Yet, in every case, these complex sounds are a compound of two primary Italian vowels:

Ö is a compound of pure E and pure O, spoken simultaneously.[4]

Ü is a compound of pure I and pure U, spoken simultaneously.[5]

Ä is a compound of pure A2 and pure E, spoken simultaneously.[6]

When you are able to isolate and pronounce perfectly these three compounded sounds, the number of vowels at your command is increased to eight. If you add the various *members* of the different vowel families, you have altogether thirteen definite vowel sounds, all of which may be isolated. With this treasure in your possession, you need not fear to study or sing in any foreign language.

We should always bear in mind the axiomatic truth that the *only* means of beautifying and improving any pure vowel is to unite it with an uninhibited breath-stream, thereby achieving the necessary *balance of resonance and breath*. The steadily flowing breath-stream (singing on the breath) is the direct result of *power working through relaxation.*[7]

---

[4] See pages 25, 51.

[5] See pages 34, 51.

[6] See pages 34, 50.

[7] See all of Chapter 10.

LESSON XV

One more preliminary step remains to be taken before the singing of text should be attempted. This is the musical application of the syllables already used as speech exercises:[1]

bE   dA   mE   nI   pO   tU   lA

Having begun the study of scales on all the fundamental Italian vowels, voice students will enjoy bending this string of syllables to music, always proceeding clockwise. They may be put to scales (later to arpeggios) in various ways, to be practiced in all comfortable keys.[2] For example:

---

[1] See page 105.

[2] Do not fail to observe the various mouth positions as you come to them!

LESSON XVI

This is an excellent "warming up" exercise. Structurally simple and comfortably rapid, it affords a quick method for moving through the entire range. It may be shortened to fit the compass of the beginner as well as lengthened to suit that of the seasoned artist.

Sing it with great vigor and gaiety, repeating each two-measure phrase *pianissimo*. *Breathe rhythmically* at the rests following each group of *staccato* notes. After inhaling at the fermata (⌢), allow the body to collapse and take a good rest before starting the return passage downward.

In this exercise, when singing the thirds *staccato,* observe the changes in mouth position of the various vowels as they occur. For instance, in measures 1, 2, and 4, A would open the mouth more on C than on E. Because a trill is too rapid to permit accurately synchronized changes in mouth positions, the first tone of any rapid trill must determine the mouth position for the remaining tones also. In measure 3, keep the open position started by C throughout the rapid trill.

Do not hesitate to shift the vowels about, thereby increasing the value of the exercise. Remember, the *vowel* dictates the mouth position.

133

LESSON XVII

The Widening Trill

Of all basic vocal exercises, the Widening Trill is one of the most useful. Some of the results following its daily practice are a smooth, even middle voice and a consciousness of *depth* and all it implies— *deep* support, *deep* breathing, motion.[1] The *principle of power working through relaxation* is *obliged* to manifest itself *completely* if you are able to sing this strenuous and exacting exercise *in tune,* if you *hear* both vowel and pitch truly.[2]

As the interval widens, *be certain* that the pitch of the upper tone does not fall, nor that of the lower tone rise. Otherwise the exercise is of no value.

Great care must be taken not to permit a "yodel" to creep into these short phrases, causing the mental picture of the phrase line to be jagged (ᴧᴧᴧᴧᴧᴧᴧᴧ). The mental picture for this exercise (indeed, for *every* phrase one sings) is a phrase-line continuous and slightly rising (————————).[3]

Lay your finger lightly upon your larynx at the front of your neck while you speak or sing a low pitch, then a high pitch. You will observe that the larynx moves from a low position to a higher one.

---

[1] See pages 70, 71, 72, 73.

[2] The Widening Trill exercise seems to *force* us back to a restatement of first principles: right feeling and right hearing as the *source* — the *cause* of right singing.

[3] I recall the natural gesture made by two of the greatest singers of the past, Calvé and Chaliapin, as they ended a phrase or a song. They slowly raised an upturned hand, timing the gesture perfectly to the duration of the phrase or tone, to the *duration of the breath.* Their bodies *never* collapsed, for, at the end of the upward moving phrase (————————), at the finish of the upward-and-outward gesture, the body waś instantly and automatically re-supplied with breath. Instinctively, these singers *"breathed into the form."* (See page 63, 2nd paragraph.)

136

For every pitch in the range of a voice, the larynx takes a special position *if not interfered with.*[4] As the intervals of the Widening Trill increase, the larynx has a greater and greater distance to travel. This can be accomplished *only* if right conditions of feeling and hearing are set up and maintained.

I have found the use of the word "smear" most helpful to pupils in attaining a perfect *legato* in any exercise. In the Widening Trill it is indispensable. *Absolutely accurate pitches* for all intervals, but an unrestricted *smear* between them!

The Widening Trill is far too difficult and exhausting for the beginner to accomplish in toto. It is enough to stop with the augmented fourth or the perfect fifth. In several months' time the distance may perhaps be increased to the octave. Progress must *never* be rushed!

The Widening Trill exercise ends with the interval of the octave —approximately E-E for high voices, D-D for middle voices, C-C for low voices. The first (minor second) interval should commence, then, about in the center of that octave, increasing either from the upper tone or the lower.

Observe the mouth positions with care during the slow (first) half of each exercise. The last half (when the rhythm is twice as fast) proceeds too rapidly for accurate synchronization. (See page 133.) Be sure to maintain a perfectly relaxed jaw, while you keep the more open position of the two tones for the remainder of the trill.

Min.2nd

Maj.2nd

Min.3rd

---

[4] See page 23, line 101.

LESSON XVIII

THE LONG ARPEGGIO

The changes of mouth positions in scale practice were slight, and very gradual. The larger intervals (thirds and fourths) of an arpeggio (broken chord) will open and close the mouth more noticeably as you proceed from tone to tone.

Preparation No. 1 for the Long Arpeggio. To be done *staccato* only. By dividing the arpeggio into sections, you will find it fairly easy to acquire precision of mouth openings.

First section. Instead of commencing to practice the following short phrase from the first tone as written (low A), try starting it on the third pitch (E), and continue it through the first note of the 2nd measure (low A). Sing these seven *staccato* notes over and over until the mouth positions (last 3 tones) come with perfect ease and accuracy. Now you will have no trouble singing the entire section from the beginning as written:

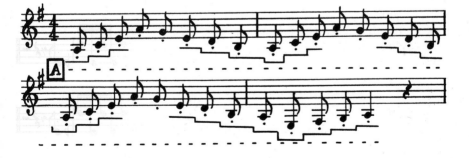

139

Second section (First inversion). Following a similar practice plan, commence this section on the third note (A, second space) and continue through seven notes, ending on low C:

Third section (Second inversion). You should have no difficulty practicing this section from the first, exactly as it is written:

You have now built the Long Arpeggio No. I in its entirety. It is to be practiced both *staccato* and *legato,* always using *rhythmic breathing* (see page 109):

Preparation No. II for the Long Arpeggio. To be practiced both *staccato* and *legato*. This is a somewhat simpler proceeding than Preparation No. I. Practice all of these sections both *staccato* and *legato*, never forgetting *rhythmic breathing:*

For variation, practice Long Arpeggio No. II in dotted rhythm, remembering *rhythmic breathing*. Dotted rhythm, rightly sung, is very good for the voice.

Dotted rhythm should be sung with great·vigor, especially during the short, *un*accented sixteenths. Do not allow the sixteenth notes to subside while you accent merely the dotted eighths! You should *feel* as though the sixteenths receive a special accent *from the body,* started at the floor into which the feet are pushing. Keep a mental picture of a continuous (not jagged), slightly rising phrase line (see page 136).

Since none of them changes mouth position in the lower portion of the range, the vowels E, I, O, and U are fairly simple to sing in arpeggios. Remember that in the case of high voices, E and O begin to open the mouth on C (third space); middle voices on B♭ or B; lowest voices on A. For I, high voices need a smile when they reach D (fourth line); middle voices at C; lowest voices at B♭.

All of the exercises in this lesson are written for high voices singing in the lowest key. Transpose them into any suitable higher keys. Middle voices may begin in the key of A♭; lowest voices in the key of G.

All the exercises in this lesson may be practiced *pianissimo* as well as with normal voice. Take pains to be accurate in differentiating between the mouth positions called for by *pianissimo* and normal voice!

LESSON XIX

This exercise looks simple enough in print, but actually, there is none more difficult to perfect.

When, after many months of practice, you are able to sing through two octaves (low A below the staff to high A above the staff) of these whole notes, absolutely according to the indicated marking (———— ————————), you will find yourself capable of studying anything written by the great composers for your type of voice.

The transition from one vowel to the next must be accomplished with perfect smoothness. There must be no "click" sound (the result of a sudden change in the shape of the throat). The quiet, harmonious activity of the *whole* body is certainly demanded by the Swell-Tone. You will find it helpful to think, just *before* every change of vowel: "Now I draw *new life* from below! *First* my body, *then* my voice!" This is especially advisable during the *decrescendo*.

It is interesting to note a characteristic peculiar to the vowel A while you are practicing the Swell-Tone. As it increases in size, it gradually opens the mouth until the maximum volume is achieved. Then, reversing the process, it gradually closes the mouth (the volume growing correspondingly less) until the original position is reached. This procedure may take place anywhere in the vocal range, irrespective of what A's normal mouth position would be at a given pitch.

143

WHAT HAPPENS INSIDE THE HEAD AND THROAT WHEN A PURE VOWEL IS PRODUCED

In each of the five plates following, the picture of what takes place inside the head and throat when a *pure vowel* is spoken[1] or sung (while *power works through relaxation* in head and body) has been indicated on the right-hand side. When an *impure vowel* is spoken or sung and *relaxation plus power* has changed to *stiffness plus impotence,* the artist has shown the resulting alterations on the left-hand side.

Each plate is a picture of the *right* way to speak or sing a vowel (when right conditions of *feeling and hearing* prevail); and each plate is also a picture of the *wrong* way to speak or sing a vowel (when wrong conditions of *feeling and hearing* prevail).

We are *always* setting up conditions of one kind or the other. These two opposites have just one thing in common—they are *absolutely consistent throughout.*

For all vowels, the normal position of the tongue is relaxed and *out* over the lower front teeth—a unit with the lower lip. The vowel itself is the formative agent, and it molds the relaxed tongue according to the pronunciation of that vowel, upon which the ear is concentrating.

---

[1] The resonance felt when *speaking* any vowel is far less intense than what the singer feels when singing that same vowel, although the *locale* of feeling is the same in both instances.

145

Right resonance feels as though it had centered itself between the nostrils and the roof of the mouth, from where it seems to reverberate throughout the entire head. We cannot *make* natural resonance by humming or by otherwise endeavoring to "place" tones. Natural resonance is a *result* over which we have no *direct* control. It is the seed of all beauty in speech and song. And *beauty always comes unsought;* it is a spontaneous thing.[2] But we certainly do *recognize* this marvelous *feeling* of resonance when it occurs. It is nature's sign of approval —like the hallmark on good silver.

If we set up and maintain right conditions of feeling[3] and listening *(right causes),* our breathing will proceed automatically and of necessity correctly *(a result)*; and our diction (also *a result*) will be understandable and meaningful in both speech and song.[4]

Concerning the five pictures of "incorrect production," the student is referred to Plates I·V .

---

[2] See page 20.
[3] See pages 69-72.
[4] See Chart, page 92.

This is a picture of our head sensations when pure A is spoken or sung. Our artist has indeed made a picture of "nasty little A"— the Beast, transformed into a wonderful Prince! (See page 115, first paragraph.)

When A is uttered, the tongue feels like a soft rug spread out over the floor of the mouth.

[5] See page 114. Also see pages 23, 61, and 77.

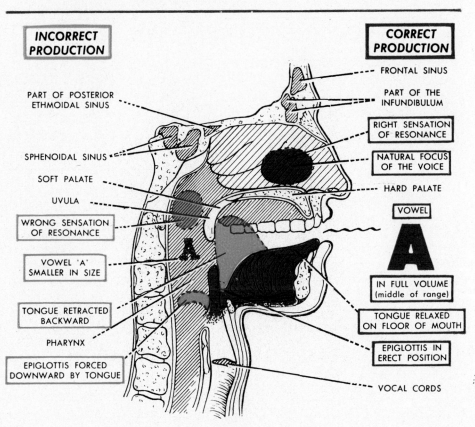

INCORRECT PRODUCTION

CORRECT PRODUCTION

PART OF POSTERIOR ETHMOIDAL SINUS

SPHENOIDAL SINUS

SOFT PALATE

UVULA

WRONG SENSATION OF RESONANCE

VOWEL 'A' SMALLER IN SIZE

TONGUE RETRACTED BACKWARD

PHARYNX

EPIGLOTTIS FORCED DOWNWARD BY TONGUE

FRONTAL SINUS

PART OF THE INFUNDIBULUM

RIGHT SENSATION OF RESONANCE

NATURAL FOCUS OF THE VOICE

HARD PALATE

VOWEL

A

IN FULL VOLUME (middle of range)

TONGUE RELAXED ON FLOOR OF MOUTH

EPIGLOTTIS IN ERECT POSITION

VOCAL CORDS

PLATE I

THE VOWEL E pronounced as in ebb[6]

This is a picture of our head sensations when pure E is spoken or sung.

The natural focus of the voice feels somewhat smaller and more packed with resonance than when A is pronounced. When we are so relaxed that a pure vowel can be uttered unimpeded and unchanged, pure E will sound extremely crude to the singer—as though an animal had taken over his vocal apparatus and were singing *through* him. This is the beginning of *beauty!*

E shapes the back of the tongue quite differently from A. It feels thick and soft and swollen, though the tip remains *out*, covering the lower front teeth and touching the lower lip.

[6] See page 120. See also pages 24, 63, and 78.

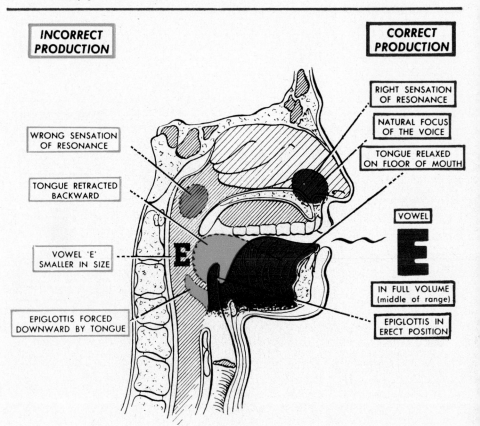

INCORRECT PRODUCTION

CORRECT PRODUCTION

RIGHT SENSATION OF RESONANCE

NATURAL FOCUS OF THE VOICE

TONGUE RELAXED ON FLOOR OF MOUTH

WRONG SENSATION OF RESONANCE

TONGUE RETRACTED BACKWARD

VOWEL

E

VOWEL 'E' SMALLER IN SIZE

IN FULL VOLUME (middle of range)

EPIGLOTTIS FORCED DOWNWARD BY TONGUE

EPIGLOTTIS IN ERECT POSITION

PLATE II

THE VOWEL I pronounced as in machine[7]

This is a picture of our head sensations when we speak or sing pure I.

If we are utterly relaxed, the vowel can shape the tongue, which *feels* even more swollen than when pure E is pronounced; in fact, it seems to quite fill both mouth and throat, and the tip remains *out* over the lower front teeth, a unit with the lower lip.

The resonance center *feels* smaller and more intensely packed than for any other vowel, and the vibrations are so strong when the I is pure that they sometimes tickle the inside lips and ears; it is as though an electric vibrator were busy inside the head.

I have found the quiet practice of the I scale (medium range, *staccato* and *legato*) of medicinal value in the case of pupils afflicted with sinus trouble. In a few minutes the breath is passing easily through the nose and a path is cleared for the free resonance of the other vowels.

[7] See page 127. See also pages 24, 63, and 79.

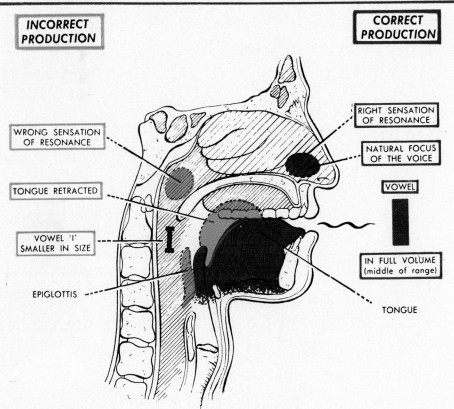

INCORRECT PRODUCTION

CORRECT PRODUCTION

WRONG SENSATION OF RESONANCE

TONGUE RETRACTED

VOWEL 'I' SMALLER IN SIZE

EPIGLOTTIS

RIGHT SENSATION OF RESONANCE

NATURAL FOCUS OF THE VOICE

VOWEL

IN FULL VOLUME (middle of range)

TONGUE

PLATE III

THE VOWEL O as pronounced by an Irish person in speaking the word "only"

This is a picture of our head sensations when we speak or sing pure O.[8] O and A have much in common both in the *feeling* of the tongue and the *feeling* of the resonance. O is a somewhat weaker vowel than A and it is sweeter in quality. The size of the resonance center is slightly smaller than that of A.

[8] See page 125. See also pages 24 64, and 79.

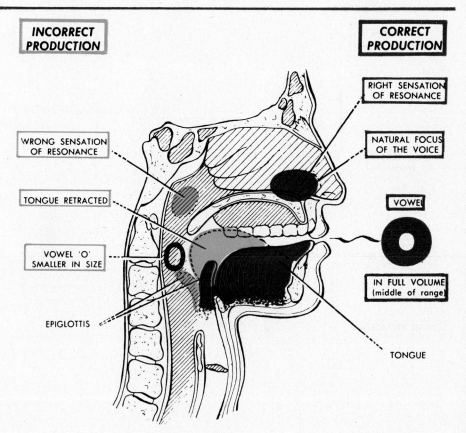

PLATE IV

THE VOWEL U pronounced as in rude

This is a picture of our head sensations when we speak or sing pure U [9]

Even though the tongue position is nearly the same as when A is uttered, U is the most closed and most *small-feeling* of all the vowels — perhaps because the resonance locale seems almost diminutive compared with that of A. That may be the reason why American singers frequently distort the pronunciation of this vowel. Unconsciously, they try to *make it sound* (to themselves) the same *size* as the other vowels. By suggesting that pure U should sound (to the singer) "no bigger than a peep-squeak." the teacher may attain the desired result in an easy way

[9] See page 129. See also pages 25, 65, and 80.

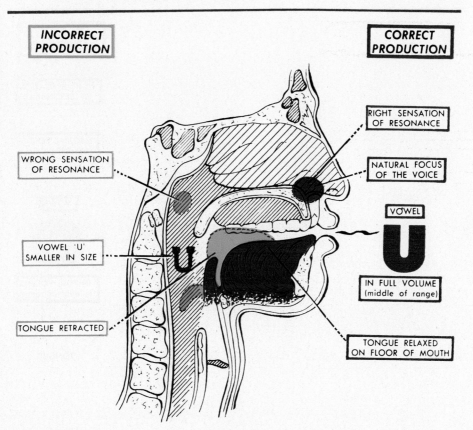

INCORRECT
PRODUCTION

CORRECT
PRODUCTION

WRONG SENSATION
OF RESONANCE

VOWEL 'U'
SMALLER IN SIZE

TONGUE RETRACTED

RIGHT SENSATION
OF RESONANCE

NATURAL FOCUS
OF THE VOICE

VOWEL

U

IN FULL VOLUME
(middle of range)

TONGUE RELAXED
ON FLOOR OF MOUTH

PLATE V

ADVICE

Never stiffen the abdomen — stomach — diaphragm!
Never stiffen the kneecaps!
Never stiffen the jaw!
Never stiffen any part of the body, inside or outside!
Never use the stroke of the glottis (snapping together of the vocal
cords) in speaking or singing!

The correct singing (or speaking) of a *staccato* tone comprises
both the correct beginning and the correct ending of any phrase. If
the starting and stopping are right, the in-between part of a phrase
stands a fair chance of being right also. The *bad habit* of commencing
staccati with a glottal attack (when a noisy "click" is heard by singer
and listener) may be overcome with comparative ease if the student
will deliberately *speak* and *hear* the consonant "h" together with each
pitch and vowel: hA hE hI hO hU. His next objective will still be
to enunciate h together with every sound he voices, but to utter it
so no one can *hear* it! Before very long the student's voice will always
be moving on the breath.[1] If his vowels are pure, breath and resonance
automatically come into balance, and he finds himself really *singing!*[2]

---

[1] See page 57.
[2] See page 82, paragraph 4.

CONCLUSION

The question is often asked: "How long a course of study is needed before a talented young singer is properly equipped and ready for a *public career?*" I am inclined to agree with Ida Auer-Herbeck that from three to four years at least are necessary, *provided the circumstances are ideal.*

"Ideal circumstances" might be defined as:

1. Perfect health.

2. The equivalent of a high school education, at least.

3. A fair musical background. (The ability to play *correctly* simple accompaniments.)

4. At least 3 lessons weekly and regularly.[1]

5. An acquaintance with Italian, German, and French.

6. At least 2 hours daily of undisturbed practice during the first 2 years of study — 2 half-hours of technique and 2 half-hours of text, new and review, with long rest periods between practice times. The daily 2 hours of work may gradually be increased to 4 hours, keeping the daily 2 half-hours of technique as a regular life habit.

---

[1] In the life of an ambitious, talented student the financial circumstances are often far from ideal. It is hoped that such difficulties may be mitigated to some extent by the *basic work* offered by this book. After a preliminary course of frequent lessons (as frequent as possible), the student should, with the help of this volume, be capable of *self instruction,* visiting the teacher once a week, or even less often.

7. The student's work in voice should be supplemented the while by thorough courses in solfège (sight singing), and varieties of body training — ballet, Mensendieck work, Dalcroze eurhythmics, etc. etc.

8. As much listening as possible to the *best* music of all kinds.

Happily, the young student's reward for undivided devotion to basic work is not slow in showing itself. Under favorable circumstances, an intelligent pupil will be singing many simple songs and arias by the end of the first year of study.

After two years of training, or even less, he may be capable of holding a not too strenuous church position.

Though it may seem unbeautiful, uninspiring and even boring to the student eager to get on to *singing,* the importance of the *basic work* in these first lessons cannot be overemphasized. This work is the foundation for all future beauty and power of expression, the foundation for which there is *no* substitute and around which there is *no* detour.

QUOTATIONS FOR SPEECH WORK

The whole cosmic scheme of life is applicable to its isolated processes. Speech output — verbal end-result of thought, differential between man and beast, index of genius or fool, characteristic of philosopher or maniac — is one of these isolated processes. (*Friedrich von Schiller*)

Art has to leave reality; it has to raise itself above bodily necessity and neediness; for art is the daughter of freedom and it requires its mandates and rules to be furnished by the necessity of spirit and not by that of matter. *Totality of character* must be found in people who are capable and worthy of exchanging the state of neediness for that of freedom. (Friedrich von Schiller's *Aesthetic Education*)

Life is display, behavior, movement, reaction. (*Anon.*)

An airplane consciousness is necessary for the appreciation of 20th-century art. (*Anon.*)

Mishaps are like knives — they either serve us or cut us, depending upon whether we grasp them by the blade or by the handle. (*Anon.*)

Wise men are not always silent, but know when to be. (*Anon.*)

To put a worth-while truth in circulation is a good day's work. (*Anon.*)

A man shows what he is by what he does with what he has. (*Anon.*)

If you confer a benefit, never remember it; if you receive one, never forget it. (*Anon.*)

It is not he who has little, but he who wants more, who is poor. (*Seneca*)

When you've written a wrathful letter, put it in the stove. (*Abraham Lincoln*)

Character is long standing habit. (*Plutarch*)

I heard the voice of the Lord saying "Whom shall I send, and who will go for us?" Then said I: "Here am I, send me." (*Isaiah 6:6*)

Start where you are with what you have; make something of it; never be satisfied. (*George Washington Carver*)

"I am still learning." (*Michelangelo's motto*)

An open mind leaves a chance for someone to drop a worth-while thought in it. (*Anon.*)

Men do not fail; they give up trying. (*Elihu Root*)

No one can work me injury but myself. (*Ralph Waldo Emerson*)

I have had more trouble with myself than with any other person I know. (*Dwight L. Moody*)

Frugality is good if liberality be joined with it. (*William Penn*)

True art brings us in contact with the divine idea, and in this sense, all true art must be sacred. The beautiful can have but one source, it can be concentrated in but one being, and this is none other than God. (*Schopenhauer*)

Training in music is tantamount to discipline, and cannot be derived from the license which acknowledges no law except this — not to be bound by any law. (*Ambros*)

Folklore is a vivid record of a people, palpitating with life itself, and its greatest art is its artlessness. It proceeds in a straight line to the significant and ignores the trivial. (*Nathan Ausubel*)

I guess the cigarette is something of a relief to paws disengaged when the human animal rose upon its feet. (*Frank Lloyd Wright*)

Each man's technique must be his own, his own way of getting his way with an idea. (*Frank Lloyd Wright*)

"Keep close to earth, my boy, and should you have to choose between truth and success, be sure to choose truth." (*Frank Lloyd Wright*)

The profound naturalness of one's own being is the essential condition of a great artist, and the condition of greatness in the man. (*Frank Lloyd Wright*)

The pen is a tricky tool — fascinating but treacherous. (*Frank Lloyd Wright*)

Nothing that happens to an individual is as important as what that individual thinks about it. (*Frank Lloyd Wright*)

Those who give largely receive largely. (*Frank Lloyd Wright*)

The truth never varies. Men's understanding of it does, and will for long, long ages to come. New knowledge brings new understanding. Hence it is that dogma dies. (*Frank Lloyd Wright*)

So long as a man seeks truth and keeps his path straight, his own *seeking* makes it true. (*Frank Lloyd Wright*)

There is no doubt that good diction is far too rare. By "diction" I mean the speaking of words correctly and easily. (*George Arliss*)

I say nothing about slang. I rather admire it; it enriches the language. But I can see no use for a lazy and careless delivery of words. (*George Arliss*)

I have said that actors must never appear to be making an effort to teach anything. But what we should do is to set a worthy example which the youth of today may be inspired to follow. And with the advent of the talking pictures our responsibility becomes far greater than ever it was before. For every person who sees an actor in the regular theater, a thousand see him when he appears in a "talky." (*George Arliss*)

In my opinion, the value of the talking screen in the improvement of the diction of the masses cannot be overestimated. Not that the masses would go to the movies to learn how to speak; but young people are inclined to be very imitative, particularly of those actors and actresses whom they especially admire. (*George Arliss*)

The man who has not anything to boast of but his illustrious ancestors is like a potato — the only good belonging to him is underground. (*Overbury*)

Many persons are more comfortable when they are dirty than when they are clean; but that does not recommend dirt as a national policy. (*George Bernard Shaw*)

The unconscious self is the real genius. Your breathing goes wrong the moment your conscious self meddles with it. (*George Bernard Shaw*)

Men are wise in proportion not to their experience, but to their capacity for experience. (*George Bernard Shaw*)

Every man is a revolutionist concerning the thing he understands. For example, every person who has mastered a profession is a skeptic concerning it, and consequently a revolutionist. (*George Bernard Shaw*)

Youth is a wonderful thing. What a crime to waste it on children! (*George Bernard Shaw*)

To this day I look to the provincial and the amateur for honesty and genuine fecundity in art. (*George Bernard Shaw*)

I have learnt that a successful revolution's first task is to shoot all revolutionists. (*George Bernard Shaw*)

Teaching, of art and everything else, was and still is so little understood by our professional instructors (mostly themselves failures) that only the ready-made geniuses make good; and even they are as often as not the worse for their academic contacts. (*George Bernard Shaw*)

When you see an unusually ornate piece of art, it is apt to be a mistake covered up. (*An old Chinese philosopher*)

If I supply you a thought, you may remember it and you may not. But if I can make you think a thought for yourself, I have indeed added to your stature. (*Epictetus*)

The man who is worthy of being a leader of men will never complain of the stupidity of his helpers, of the ingratitude of mankind, nor of the inappreciation of the public. These things are all a part of the great game of life, and to meet them and not go down before them in discouragement and defeat is the final proof of power. (*Elbert Hubbard*)

Folks who never do any more than they get paid for, never get paid for any more than they do. (*Elbert Hubbard*)

The best service a book can render you is, not to *impart* truth, but to make you think it out for yourself. (*Elbert Hubbard*)

Education is simply the encouragement of right habits — the fixing of good habits until they become a part of one's nature, and are exercised automatically. (*Elbert Hubbard*)

Life consists of molting our illusions. We form creeds today only to throw them away tomorrow. The eagle molts a feather because he is growing a better one. (*Elbert Hubbard*)

I believe that no one can harm us but ourselves; that sin is misdirected energy; that there is no devil but fear; and that the universe is planned for good. Winter is as necessary as Summer, Night is as useful as Day, and Death is a manifestation of Life, and just as good. (*Elbert Hubbard*)

The heroic man does not pose; he leaves that for the man who wishes to be thought heroic. (*Elbert Hubbard*)

Conscience is chiefly fear of society, or fear of oneself. (*D. H. Lawrence*)

Money poisons you when you've got it and starves you when you haven't. (*D. H. Lawrence*)

You can't insure against the future, except by really believing in the best bit of you, and in the power beyond it. (*D. H. Lawrence*)

Falsehoods not only disagree with truth, but also quarrel among themselves. (*Daniel Webster*)

The only limit to our realization of tomorrow will be our doubts

of today. LET US MOVE FORWARD WITH STRONG AND AC-
TIVE FAITH. (*Franklin Delano Roosevelt's last message to America*)

Faith keeps us on the growing edge of life. (*Ralph W. Sockman*)

The greatest joy in life is the joy of giving joy. (*Ralph W. Sockman*)

A friend reveals new possibilities in us and shows us stars we
never saw before. (*Ralph W. Sockman*)

Friendship is a sentiment cooler than passion and warmer than
respect, which recognizes a kindred spirit in another person. (*Ralph
W. Sockman*)

In our desire to be sincere and genuine, let us not mistake raw-
ness for realism. (*Ralph W. Sockman*)

In life, those who do not try are left behind. (From *Fifth Chinese
Daughter*)

When an individual from a minority group personally succeeds,
he too often turns his back on his own group. (From *Fifth Chinese
Daughter*)

The moment of triumph is always very dangerous. Because you
believe that you have made your book, your picture, your drama,
your symphony, your victory. Poor fool! Poor fool! Do you not
realize that you are merely the glove upon the hand of God? (*James
Francis Cooke*)

If we had paid no more attention to our plants than we have to
our children, we would now be living in a jungle of weeds. (*Luther
Burbank*)

Solitude is as needful to the imagination as society is wholesome
to the character. (*James Russell Lowell*)

To love and win is the best thing; to love and lose, the next best.
(*William Makepeace Thackeray*)

There is but one God — is it Allah or Jehovah? The palm-tree is sometimes called a date-tree, but there is only one tree. (*Benjamin Disraeli*)

A great thing is a great book; but a greater thing than all is the talk of a great man. (*Benjamin Disraeli*)

It is much easier to be critical than to be correct. (*Benjamin Disraeli*)

The art of conversation is to be prompt without being stubborn, to refute without argument, and to clothe great matters in a motley garb. (*Benjamin Disraeli*)

A man is an animal that writes. (*Homer*)

Ignorance is the night of the mind, but a night without moon or star. (*Confucius*)

Forty is the old age of youth; fifty is the youth of old age. (*Victor Hugo*)

The ladder of life is full of splinters, but they always prick the hardest when we're sliding down. (*William L. Brownell*)

He who loveth a book will never want a faithful friend, a wholesome counsellor, a cheerful companion, or an effectual comforter. (*Isaac Barrow*)

The men who try to do something and fail are infinitely better than those who try to do nothing and succeed. (*Lloyd Jones*)

You cannot believe in honor until you have achieved it. Better keep yourself clean and bright; you are the window through which you must see the world. (*George Bernard Shaw*)

Men, even when alone, lighten their labor by song, however rude it may be. (*Quintillian*)

Habit is a cable; we weave a thread of it every day, and at last we cannot break it. (*Horace Mann*)

Every man's life is a fairy tale written by God's fingers. (*Hans Christian Andersen*)

Art is more godlike than science. Science discovers; art creates. (*John Opie*)

I envy the beasts two things — their ignorance of evil to come and their ignorance of what is said about them. (*Voltaire*)

Originality is merely a pair of fresh eyes. (*T. W. Higginson*)

The highest and most lofty trees have the most reason to dread the thunder. (*Charles Rollin*)

Quiet minds cannot be perplexed or frightened, but go on in fortune or misfortune at their own private pace, like a clock during a thunderstorm. (*Robert Louis Stevenson*)

The only true happiness we may look for comes from squandering ourselves for a purpose. (*John Mason Brown*)

Only the weak are obliged to be violent; the strong, having all means at command, need not resort to the worst. Refined art is not wanting in power if the public is refined also. (*George Santayana*)

To find a career to which you are adapted by nature, and then to work hard at it, is about as near to a formula for success and happiness as the world provides. One of the fortunate aspects of this formula is that, granted the right career has been found, the hard work takes care of itself. Then hard work is not hard work at all. (*Mark Sullivan*)